PENGUIN

THE APPRENTICE TOURIST

MÁRIO DE ANDRADE (1893–1945) was a Brazilian writer, born in São Paulo, best known for the gleefully anarchic rhapsody *Macunaíma: The Hero with No Character* (1928). A polymath of his era, he was trained as a musician but became equally influential in fiction, poetry, photography, and art criticism. He served as the founding director of São Paulo's Department of Culture and helped organize and participated in the Semana de Arte Moderna (Week of Modern Art) in 1922, an event that would be central to the birth of modernism in Brazil. A key thread of Andrade's work involved the recognition and preservation of Afro-Brazilian cultures and traditions.

FLORA THOMSON-DeVEAUX is a translator, writer, and researcher whose translation of *The Posthumous Memoirs of Brás Cubas* by Machado de Assis was acclaimed as "a gift to scholars" by *The New York Times*. She studied Spanish and Portuguese at Princeton University and earned a PhD in Portuguese and Brazilian studies from Brown University. She lives in Rio de Janeiro.

MÁRIO DE ANDRADE

The Apprentice Tourist

TRAVELS ALONG THE AMAZON TO PERU,
ALONG THE MADEIRA TO BOLIVIA,
AND AROUND MARAJÓ BEFORE SAYING
ENOUGH ALREADY

Translated with an Introduction and Notes by
FLORA THOMSON-DeVEAUX

PENGUIN BOOKS

PENGUIN BOOKS
An imprint of Penguin Random House LLC
penguinrandomhouse.com

Originally published in 1976 in Portuguese as *O turista aprendiz* by Duas Cidades, São Paulo

All photographs are from the Arquivo do Instituto de Estudos Brasileiros USP—Fundo Mário de
Andrade with the following reference codes: (page 13) MA-F-0159; (page 19, top) MA-F-0175;
(page 19, bottom) MA-F-0184; (page 27) MA-F-0205; (page 37) MA-F-0237;
(page 38) MA-F-0254; (page 46) MA-F-0259; (page 59) MA-F-0293; (page 78, left)
MA-F-0341; (page 78, right) MA-F-0340; (page 98, top) MA-F-0411;
(page 98, bottom) MA-F-0417; (page 138) MA-F-0542.

Maps by Joana Lavôr

LIBRARY OF CONGRESS CATALOGING-IN-PUBLICATION DATA
Names: Andrade, Mário de, 1893–1945, author. | Thomson-DeVeaux, Flora,
translator, writer of introduction.
Title: The apprentice tourist / Mário de Andrade ; translated with an introduction
and notes by Flora Thomson-DeVeaux.
Other titles: Turista aprendiz. English
Description: New York : Penguin Books, [2023] | Originally published in
1976 in Portuguese as O turista aprendiz by Duas Cidades, São Paulo.
Identifiers: LCCN 2022030787 (print) | LCCN 2022030788 (ebook) |
ISBN 9780143137351 (paperback) | ISBN 9780593511305 (ebook)
Subjects: LCSH: Brazil—Description and travel. | Andrade, Mário de,
1893–1945—Diaries. | Andrade, Mário de, 1893–1945—Travel—Brazil. |
Authors, Brazilian—20th century—Biography. | LCGFT: Travel writing.
Classification: LCC F2515 .A51813 2023 (print) | LCC F2515 (ebook) |
DDC 918.1/045—dc19/eng/20220705
LC record available at https://lccn.loc.gov/2022030787
LC ebook record available at https://lccn.loc.gov/2022030788

Printed in the United States of America
1st Printing

Set in Sabon LT Pro
Designed by Sabrina Bowers

Cover art collage: Eleanor Shakespeare
Cover images: (photo details) Archive of the Institute of Brazilian Studies
USP – Fundo Mário de Andrade (reference codes: MA-F-0236, MA-F-0514, MA-F-0547,
MA-F-0577, MA-F-0615, MA-F-0633, MA-MMA-080-013, MA-MMA-080-216);
bromeliad flower, Grafissimo / Getty Images

Contents

THE APPRENTICE TOURIST

Introduction

Travel is the traveler. What we see isn't what we see but what we are.

—Fernando Pessoa, tr. Richard Zenith

Happy travelers are all alike; each unhappy traveler is unhappy in their own way. And few unhappy travelers finding themselves out of joint and out of place are as interesting as Mário de Andrade in the Amazon.

"Since Sunday, my life's done a somersault," he wrote in a letter to a friend. After years of dreaming about Amazonia, he'd decided at the last minute to embark on a three-month odyssey up the great river—and "to hell with this hellish life" in São Paulo. He had been saving up for everything but this: there was a new book of poetry to be published and a long-planned trip across the Brazilian Northeast. But the invitation proved irresistible. After a few sleepless nights, Andrade borrowed money from his brother and got time off from the conservatory where he taught. The year was 1927.

It was to be an expedition of writers and modernist thinkers into the heart of the Brazilian rainforest. When Andrade showed up on the dock in Rio de Janeiro, however, clutching a cane that he vaguely imagined as a defensive weapon against alligators and fire ants, he was in for a disappointment. "Everyone had flown the coop! It's just me, Dona Olívia, and the two girls." Dona Olívia was the São Paulo society lady and patron of the arts who had put the trip together, the two girls were her niece and a friend, and Andrade was the only illustrious guest who'd followed through on the invitation. At that point, however, it was too late to escape.

At age thirty-three, Mário Raul Morais de Andrade had been the gravitational center of São Paulo's artistic vanguard, whether he liked it or not—and he mostly did—for the better part of a decade. He had published several books of poetry, including the tremendously influential *Pauliceia desvairada* (Hallucinated City), which pioneered one of his literary hallmarks: the insistence on writing Portuguese as it was really spoken in Brazil, not the high-flown language taught from European-influenced grammars. In 1922, he was chief among the organizers of the São Paulo Modern Art Week, an event meant to serve as ground zero for the modernist movement in Brazil.

As European artists drew inspiration from the "primitive" aesthetics of the tropics, their Brazilian colleagues were driven to do the same—the key difference being that their inspiration came from a rediscovery of their own land. A hundred years after the nation's independence from Portugal, Brazilian modernism emerged as a playful, acerbic rejection of arts in a Belle Époque mold and an attempt to rediscover and highlight Indigenous and non-Portuguese elements of the nation's culture, a shift with a seismic impact on the arts in all fields. In a group of brilliant minds, Andrade emerged as a leader and came to be referred to as the Pope of Brazilian modernism, although he detested the nickname (one friend urged him to just relax and "accept the Papacy").

In subsequent years, Andrade began dedicating himself more seriously to the study of Brazilian folk culture. While *Hallucinated City* includes paeans to São Paulo, his frenetic hometown, Andrade had begun looking toward the regions of Brazil that were so different from the Paulista metropolis as to push any concept of shared nationhood to the breaking point. In "Descobrimento" (The Discovery), written in 1925, he pictures himself sitting at his desk at home before an open book, struck by a chill and a revelation:

I remembered that up there in the North, my God! so far away
   from me
In the blinding darkness of fallen night
A pale thin man, hair running into his eyes
Having made a lump of the day's rubber,
Has only just lain down, and is asleep.

That man is a Brazilian just like me.

Then, in "Acalanto do seringueiro" (Lullaby for a Rubber Tapper), the companion poem to "Descobrimento," the poet strains to reach out to his imagined compatriot, dozing in the westernmost state in Brazil:

What must the darkness be like
Out in the virgin forest in Acre?
And what about the aromas,
The softness or roughness
Of the soil that I call mine too?
How poor I am! I can't hear
The note sung by the uirapuru . . .
I have to see secondhand,
Feel through what they tell me,
You, rubber tapper out in Acre,
Just as Brazilian as me
In the darkness of the forest,
Sleep, tapper, sleep.

The ultimate expression of this yearning to embrace an idea of nationhood would be *Macunaíma: o herói sem nenhum caráter* (Macunaíma: The Hero with No Character), the genre-bending work that Andrade dubbed a "rhapsody," which follows a shapeshifting Indigenous (anti)hero from the rainforest to the equally baffling landscapes of urban Brazil and back. He wrote the bulk of it in 1926, in a six-day frenzy at a friend's farm, fueled by cigarettes and lulled by the sway of a hammock, without ever having set foot in the tropical landscapes he brought to life. Not that the idea was to faithfully depict the jungles of Brazil—on the contrary, the book is what he called a gleefully "de-geographized" hodgepodge of flora, fauna, slang, historical figures, and landmarks from all across Brazil, almost nothing placed where it "ought" to be.

The invitation to travel from Rio de Janeiro to the western frontier, steaming up the Amazon and the Madeira, came as Andrade was revising *Macunaíma*, which would be published the following year. He was the first to admit that he was no great traveler. Even as colleague after colleague made their seemingly inevitable transatlantic pilgrimages, and friends exhorted him to set sail for Paris or risk never understanding the modern world, Andrade bristled and stayed put. Although he spent most of his adult life peppered with invitations to visit Europe and to give talks in the United States, Argentina, and elsewhere, he only ever set foot outside Brazil on the brief occasions narrated here—a few days in Peru and an afternoon in Bolivia. The trip through Amazonia would be one of the few grand journeys of his life.

Andrade set out from São Paulo on May 7, 1927, and returned on August 15. The route is in the title: *The Apprentice Tourist: Travels along the Amazon to Peru, along the Madeira to Bolivia, and around Marajó before Saying Enough Already* (a parody, among other long-winded travelogue titles, of the 1883 *Travel Notes from São Paulo to the Capital of Goiás, from there to that of Pará, along the Araguaia, Tocantins, and Pará Rivers to the Court: Administrative and Political Reflections*, by his maternal grandfather Joaquim de Almeida Leite Morais). They went by train and steamer, canoe and "dustmobile": by train from São Paulo to Rio, then steaming up the coast to Belém do Pará at the mouth of the Amazon, from there up the great river to Iquitos in Peru, back down past Manaus and up the Madeira River, all the way to the Bolivian frontier, then back down the Madeira, the Amazon, Marajó Island, and the Brazilian coast. Andrade had no say in the itinerary, which may have been designed to serve the business interests of its organizer, Olívia Penteado, whom he nicknamed the "Coffee Queen," and to whom he played second fiddle throughout the trip. (On the one occasion when a local authority made a speech specifically welcoming him, he was almost taken aback.)

Andrade's ambivalence toward both travel and the process of capturing it in the written word is part of what makes *The Apprentice Tourist* so remarkable. Like so many of us, he is torn between fully experiencing a place and mentally transforming it into narration—but unlike so many of us, he is armed with a formidable mental library of literary references that both enrich and cloud his vision. Seeing things firsthand, rather than through the words of others, proves more complicated than it might seem. The travelogue is shot through with allusions to previous chroniclers of tropical Brazil, from José de Alencar to Pêro Vaz de Caminha to Euclides da Cunha, and dotted with a similarly "de-geographized" array of references to everything from Dante to Bocage. Andrade's long-harbored desire to visit the region functions alternately as poison and cure: while he is frustrated with his inability to see anything "useful" for literary purposes, that frustration makes the trip's moments of serendipity, when they come, all the brighter.

The paradox of travel writing seems encapsulated in the entry on June 7, describing the great Amazonian water lily: the act of description has the same effect as the traveler who rows out to the flower, cuts its stem, and lifts the great blossom up, "ruining the whole thing a bit" in the process. Andrade, one of the most prodigious and finest letter writers that Brazilian literature has known, dispatched only a single letter to his friend and fellow poet Manuel Bandeira, during the trip, and confessed that the process left him "sadder than you could ever imagine."

> I'm taking a few notes here and there, but I don't think anything will come out of this trip. You can sense when there's something to be made of what you're feeling. This time, I can't sense anything. More and more, ecstasy is taking over. I've given myself up with a sensuousness I'd never known to the contemplation of things, and that means I haven't got the slightest control over

myself. Intelligence has no tools to react even the tiny bit one would need to systematize in data or in conscious thought what the senses are taking in.

That "sensuous contemplation of things" goes for a more corporeal sensuality as well as a rapturous observation of the landscape. Andrade coyly reports on flirtations with women throughout the book, from a wordless exchange with an American woman who, he claims, "devoted me her eternal love, but was forced to stay in Bahia since I can't afford any entanglements" to a kiss from a Chinese woman named Glória: "She had a name that didn't belong to her, and it was impossible for me to kiss her back." His most constant companions on the trip were ultimately "the two girls," the young women accompanying Olívia Penteado: Margarida Guedes Nogueira and Dulce do Amaral Pinto, ages nineteen and twenty-one, whom he hides behind the nicknames Scales and Trumpet in the text. At multiple points in the book, Andrade jokes half seriously about pangs of jealousy when they flirt with handsome locals who venture onto the boat. The curiosity was mutual: Andrade's biographer Jason Tércio reports that the girls took a penknife to the wall separating their cabin from his and carved out a little hole to spy on him from time to time, finding that he was almost always writing.

Among Andrade's vast unfinished oeuvre is *Balança, Trombeta e Battleship: ou o descobrimento da alma* (Scales, Trumpet, and Battleship: Or the Discovery of the Soul), which he first sketched out on the few remaining pages of a notebook from the 1927 trip. In this novella, an English pickpocket named Battleship disembarks in Rio and comes to care for two urchin girls, Scales and Trumpet. Its climax—the "discovery of the soul"—is a sequence in which Battleship decides to scrub the two girls down in a stream, and the bashfulness of one of the girls strips all of them of their virginity, in an emotional rather than a physical sense. Andrade fleshed out the story over the course of the 1930s; a fragment would be published in 1940, but the full (albeit incomplete) text was published in

1994, thanks to Telê Ancona Lopez of the University of São Paulo.

A conspiracy of would-be polite silence has long shrouded Andrade's sexuality, but reports from contemporaries, as well as a letter kept under lock and key until 2015 in which he addresses the subject more or less directly, indicate that he was queer—he once referred to it as a sort of "pansexuality." Oswald de Andrade (no relation), the writer in whose company Mário rejoiced when he intercepted the travelers on their return to Rio de Janeiro, would, during one burn-all-bridges phase a few years later, pen potshots referring to his colleague as "Miss São Paulo" and "Miss Macunaíma." The extent to which Mário de Andrade allowed himself to pursue same-sex desires, however, is unclear. In "Federico Paciência," a short story rewritten obsessively over the course of decades and only published posthumously, he paints an aching portrait of a passionate, ultimately stymied relationship between two teenage boys. Ultimately, desire itself, regardless of its object, seemed to be too heavy a burden to bear. On more than one occasion on the trip through Amazonia, upon observing the listless indifference of people suffering from malaria, he recorded an aching to come down with the same disease, "so nothing would ever interest me, in this world in which everything interests me far more than it should . . ."

The issue of Andrade's racial identification is no less ambiguous. He was darker than his parents and siblings, and once recalled having been targeted with jeers of *negro!* by virtue of what he called his "doubtful" skin color, this presumably in São Paulo. However, in Amazonia he was marked unquestionably as a white outsider: "In Tefé the Portuguese man from the shop swore I was Portuguese born and bred, in Tonantins I passed for Italian, and now, here in São Paulo de Olivença, Brother Fidélis asks me hesitantly if I'm English or German!"

The Apprentice Tourist oscillates between rapturous description and sarcastic, down-to-earth diary entries, ranging from the indignities of "baths" with cachaça to the fact that the same terrible movie was being shown in nearly every town the expedition visited, priceless descriptions of a landscape since transformed and now threatened with utter extinction—accompanied by copious photographs taken by the author himself, a selection of which appears in this edition—and disorienting flights of fancy that include ethnographies invented from whole cloth. Having exhaustively studied anthropologists' and explorers' accounts of the lives and cosmologies of multiple Indigenous peoples in Brazil, Andrade was anxious to have direct contact with communities throughout the Amazon—so anxious, in fact, that he recorded a stress dream about delivering a speech in Tupi and being told in no uncertain terms that it was "all wrong." The fear was misplaced, in a sense: rather, his desire to engage with Indigenous peoples would be persistently thwarted over the course of the trip, reduced to a few fleeting, unsatisfactory interactions.

In a sort of literary revenge, then, Andrade began concocting credulity-stretching reports on his expeditions to Indigenous villages. In a pompous pseudoscientific tone, he informs his readers of his visit to the Pacaás Novos, who believe that the most shameful parts of the body are the face and mouth, consider speech to be as intimate as we do sexual relations, and communicate through kicks and wiggling their toes; and to the Do-Mi-So Indians, who convey meaning through musical phrases and proudly trace their heritage back to sloths. The effect is Swiftian, all the more so when one considers how little most people knew then and know now about the hundreds of Indigenous peoples who call Brazilian territory home. (It says something that the other day, upon hearing the details of one of these "ethnographies," a well-informed person asked cautiously if the Pacaás Novos still observed those customs. They do not, nor have they ever.)

"In these 'notes on my journey,' as my grandfather Leite Morais called them, I often hesitate to recount certain things for fear I won't be believed," Andrade wrote with a wink. In describing Amerigo Vespucci's profoundly flawed but bestselling chronicle of the New World, John Hemming quips that the chronically unreliable navigator must have been "the patron saint of all travel writers." While Andrade's inadvertent inaccuracies are few, and I have attempted to correct them whenever possible, his deliberate exaggerations, playful distortions, and flat-out fibs place him squarely in the long, illustrious lineage of people who went to the Amazon and then stretched the truth about what they did and saw there.

Even after centuries of exploration and study, Amazonia is slow to reveal its secrets and still toes the line between fact and fantastical—and *The Apprentice Tourist* takes full advantage of that confusion. Yes, apuís do wrap around other trees and strangle them to death, and yes, native bees do make their hives in the hollows left by the rotted-out trunks; but no, the Brazilian government did not install a little faucet to dispense the resulting honey. Even having studied the book at length and traveled down a part of the Amazon, I was caught off guard at certain points. I had thought that Andrade's description of certain sloths as "quite rushed" was just a joke. It may well have been, but I was chagrined to hear from a guide in Manaus that the *preguiça-real*, the southern two-toed sloth, is "the devil incarnate": not only can it move rather quickly, but it also has a nasty temper. And while Andrade scoffs at one Peruvian's tall tales of twelve-meter alligators, a prehistoric crocodilian called *Purussaurus brasiliensis* once stalked Amazonia, weighing several tons and clocking in at very close to Dr. Vigil's description. So as not to spoil Andrade's fun, I've largely refrained from fact-checking him here: but readers beware, here be both tall tales and implausible truths.

Even as it provides the entertainment afforded by literature's best travel diaries, *The Apprentice Tourist* also embarks on another sort of journey entirely. A few days in, Andrade reflected on the sensations of the trip up the coast: "There's a sort of stubborn feeling of not-enoughness . . . that absolutely wrecks the neat gray European I still have in me." As the steamer makes its way upriver, he is driven to rethink the nation in which he lives and subvert its ingrained Eurocentrism—a task pioneered by the modernist movement and made even more urgent today, as the forests that knocked Andrade off his feet (on one occasion, literally) are being reduced to ash.

Since the election of Jair Bolsonaro in 2018, Brazil has seen a full-throated endorsement of the predatory exploitation of the Amazon, from massive fires set to clear pastures for cattle and soybean plantations to the illegal (but tolerated) harvesting of lumber from old-growth forests and brutal attacks on Indigenous peoples on what ought to be their protected lands. In late 2021, at the very bend of the Madeira River where Andrade described "the smell of a forest in flower, a wild smell, warm, luscious," a horrific sight made headlines across the world: a flotilla of illegal barges dredging for gold had materialized, nearly spanning the vast river from shore to shore. A month earlier, a similar dredging operation on the Uraricoera River had sucked two Yanomami boys into the machinery of a barge, drowning them.

Nearly a century on, as Brazil's natural landscape and Indigenous peoples are suffering such terrible blows in the name of shortsighted gains, Andrade's musings ring all the clearer. "We take pride in being the only great (great?) civilized country in the tropics," he wrote. "This is the flaw in us. . . . We ought to think and feel like Indians, Chinese, folks from Benin, Java. . . . Perhaps then we might be able to create a culture and civilization of our own. At least we'd be more us, I'm sure of that."

For the twentieth anniversary of the São Paulo Modern Art Week, in 1942, Andrade was invited to give a talk. In it, he delivered not a self-satisfied retrospective of the birth of the modernist movement but rather a disillusioned critique. While recognizing the importance and influence of modernism, he observed the ways in which its nonconformist aesthetic had been used to paper over conventional creations. Moreover, he looked sternly on his own work, as well as that of his contemporaries, in which he identified a degree of dilettantism, a juvenile tendency to attack the wrong targets, and above all, an overweening individualism at a time that called for the "political and social improvement of man." This may shed further light on the ambiguous sentiments in the preface, in which Andrade declares that *The Apprentice Tourist* has aged over the years and "wafts of modernism," but can't bring himself to

destroy it. He had no such qualms about many other manuscripts, making us all the more fortunate.

In response to a questionnaire sent by the publishing house
Macaulay, most likely on the occasion of the English translation of his novel *Amar, verbo intransitivo*—it was released as
Fräulein in 1933—Andrade explained: "I write several books
at once, such that I'm able to take refuge from the worries of
one in another." *The Apprentice Tourist*, as one may glean
from its rather fretful preface, seemed to have caused significant worry, and so he took refuge in other projects rather than
publish it straightaway. But there were other factors: as he patiently explained in response to Macaulay's questions, "In Brazil, it is still rare for a writer to be able to make a living off his
books." Andrade was certainly no exception: apart from his
job at the São Paulo Conservatory, he would later teach at a
university in Rio, have an intensely productive tenure as the director of São Paulo's Department of Culture, and constantly
write articles and essays on commission.

Having published a few excerpts from his Amazonian diary
in the few years following the trip, Andrade sat down to thoroughly revise it only in late 1943. Before he could arrive at a
final draft and publish it, however, he died of a heart attack in
February 1945, at age fifty-one. *O turista aprendiz* was first
made available to the Brazilian public in full in 1976, in an edition compiled by the indefatigable Telê Ancona Lopez. It included both the diary from Andrade's 1927 trip and notes from
a subsequent tour of the Brazilian Northeast in 1928–1929,
this one much more along the lines of what he had originally
imagined for his Amazonian sojourn: unburdened by polite
company and able to dive into the task of collecting folklore
and music. This translation limits itself to the Amazonian
journey—in part because of the disarming "personal nature"
of the first diaries, as the author describes it somewhat despair-
ingly, which is precisely what makes them all the more memor-
able and relatable.

Each edition of *The Apprentice Tourist* to date has taken a
slightly different approach to the text, and this one is no exception. Andrade left behind a vibrant travelogue, but the

typescript presents some loose ends: multiple versions of certain passages, little fables composed after the fact and never incorporated into the body of the diary, inconclusive marginal musings on whether to include a given story in May or July, and so on. This translation takes its lead from the 1943 typescript in the archives of the Instituto de Estudos Brasileiros and has included the loose fables in an appendix at the end of the travelogue. Hanging over any attempt to arrive at a definitive version of the text, however, is this annotation on one page of the typescript in Andrade's cramped cursive: *"These jottings are not to be published, they're just notes for a book that would be nothing of the sort."*

As an apprentice tourist, Andrade struggled to let his guard down, ultimately concluding, "I was sunk in myself all along that broad watery road." In these "jottings," we find a poet in the Amazon trying to wrest an indomitable world into words: the inconceivable scale of the river mouth, the mercurial colors of dawn on the Madeira, the poetry of a duck being devoured by an alligator in a single snap.

FLORA THOMSON-DeVEAUX

A Note on the Translation

Mário de Andrade's prose is unfailingly radical, in ways both subtle and obvious. Throughout *The Apprentice Tourist*, Andrade favors a deliberate colloquiality, both as an attempt to bridge the abyss between spoken and written Brazilian Portuguese and as a creeping affectation. This includes the "incorrect" inflection of *meio* (sort of) to the feminine *meia* and the abbreviated spellings of *para o* and *para a* as *pra* and *pro* (common in informal Portuguese writing to this day), *guspir* instead of *cuspir*, and the free use of hyphens, among other idiosyncrasies. Wherever possible, I've attempted to imagine what Andrade might have wrought in English, and have thus used "tho" instead of "though"—surely he would've scorned the silent "ugh"—and "s'posed" for "supposed," as well as following his lead when he smashes words together and ventures into neologisms, such as *fotar* ("We photoed the tame margay") rather than *fotografar*. The strangeness is often unobtrusive—a swapped-out preposition here, a syntax that seems normal at first glance but blossoms into near incomprehension upon further inspection. As I translated, I'd often find a phrase peculiar, throw it into a search engine, and discover that it seemed to be the only registered occurrence in written Portuguese. Andrade's inventiveness was a constant source of dismay, amusement, and awe.

In approaching the flora and fauna that populate the book, I have attempted to keep the text as colloquial as possible without betraying botanical and zoological precision. In a few cases I made up English common names to match their colorful Portuguese equivalents, lest the reader be deprived of understanding or put at arm's length by a scientific name. One notable exception to strict fidelity is *jacaré*, an animal whose name rings familiar to any Brazilian but whose English equivalent, "caiman," has an off-puttingly zoological air. May the jacarés forgive me for dressing them up as alligators (they belong to the Alligatoridae family, in my defense), and may I be spared their revenge the next time I find myself in Amazonian waters.

And since this landscape will be as unimaginably foreign to many readers as it was to Andrade, I recognize that when reading the words tinamou, margay, and pirarucu, you may be understandably hard-pressed to pick out which is the diminutive jungle cat, which the massive river fish, and which the plump little bird. Aleijadinho, the masterful mixed-race sculptor whom Andrade adored, worked in the high mining country of Minas Gerais during the Baroque. When called upon to depict the lions that threatened the prophet Daniel's life, he was stumped for a reference, being perhaps familiar with jaguars at most; and the resulting "lions" are peculiar but charming curly-maned creatures with monkey faces and hawklike talons. If you feel inspired to look up the creatures that Andrade spotted, you'll be in for a cornucopia of riotously colored birds, flowers, and fish; but if you prefer to imagine your own tinamous, margays, and pirarucus, I'm sure the author would approve.

Occasionally Andrade misheard the names of communities along his route, and whenever possible I have adjusted the spelling so as to help readers follow along on whatever map they may be consulting. Likewise, I corrected a few errors in his transcriptions of dialogues in Spanish and have rectified the spelling of the Huitoto (also Witoto) people's name, which appears in the original and subsequent publications as Huitota (the feminine adjective form).

A note on exchange rates: At the time of Mário de Andrade's journey, one mil-réis was officially worth twelve cents of a dollar. I have glossed the next unit up, the conto, in terms of thousands of mil-réis, since one conto was worth one thousand mil-réis. The relative worth of purchases is fairly easy to deduce throughout the text, as the author notes the pittance paid to the men who load firewood onto the ship (two mil-réis for carrying a thousand logs) and raises a disbelieving eyebrow at a fellow passenger who claims to have spent nine hundred mil-réis on his suit.

I would be remiss if I didn't acknowledge the role of Pedro Meira Monteiro and André Botelho in the development of this translation. They encouraged me to translate an initial sample of the text in 2019—our dream, sadly scrapped by the pandemic, was to retrace some portion of Andrade's trip—and have been invaluable interlocutors ever since, helping puzzle through invented slang, nonexistent birds, and mystifying prepositions.

The translation process was bookended by visits to Amazonia—one trip down the Amazon from Santarém to Belém and stops along the upper reaches of the Rio Negro and the area around Manaus—on which I was able to grasp at hints of Andrade's experience. The Madeira-Mamoré railway on which he rode is a distant memory, as are the steamers and their passengers; but even a century on, a traveler armed with pen and notebook whose boat approaches a curve in the Amazon, filling the view ahead with an impenetrable mass of stunning greens, may easily sense the landscape bubbling up with "living mysteries" and "feel that the revelation is bound to come—grandiose, terrible, just around the river bend." The revelation, this time around, may be just how much remains to be done to preserve those living mysteries.

Suggestions for Further Reading

Despite Mário de Andrade's monumental importance to Brazilian literature, his works have been slow to find recognition in the English-speaking world, often hobbled by tardy or faltering translations. *Pauliceia desvairada*, the poetry collection that laid the foundations for Brazilian modernism, was translated in 1968 by Jack E. Tomlins as *Hallucinated City* (Vanderbilt University Press). *Macunaíma*, his magnum opus, was brought into English only in 1984, half a century after its publication, in an almost unrecognizable rendition by E. A. Goodland (Random House)—a literary wrong on its way to being righted by Katrina Dodson's lively new translation (New Directions, 2023). His 1927 novel, *Amar, verbo intransitivo*, has been translated twice, first in a considerably abridged and adapted version by Margaret Richardson Hollingsworth, under the title *Fräulein* (Macaulay, 1933), and more recently by Ana Lessa-Schmidt as *To Love, Intransitive Verb* (New London Librarium, 2018). A handful of his short stories have been translated over the years; five are included in *Short Stories by Mário de Andrade*, a bilingual edition published by Unicamp in 2020 in a translation by John Ellis. Much of his poetry, to say nothing of his writings on Brazilian music and folklore, remains untranslated.

Readers of *The Apprentice Tourist*, having been exposed to Mário de Andrade's take on Amazonia, may enjoy a stroll through some of his predecessors' impressions. *The Brazil Reader* (Duke University Press, 2019), edited by James N. Green, Victoria Langland, and Lilia M. Schwarcz, includes more than a hundred translated and contextualized documents from throughout the nation's history, the first of which is Pêro Vaz de Caminha's "Letter to King Manuel I of Portugal," the scrivener's account often mythologized as "Brazil's birth certificate" and to which Andrade, thrust into the role of discoverer of his own land, refers indirectly throughout his diaries. While it describes an encounter between the Portuguese and Indigenous peoples on the coast of what is now the northeastern state of Bahia, and not in the Amazon, it marks the inauguration of a series of tropes about the tropics and its people that still echo today.

Euclides da Cunha, best known for his searing account of a messianic movement crushed by the Brazilian army in 1897 (translated as *Rebellion in the Backlands* by Samuel Putnam and *Backlands: The Canudos Campaign* by Elizabeth Lowe), also traveled to the Amazon, in 1905, as part of a joint expedition to fix the border between Brazil and Peru. He chronicled the journey in a book published posthumously, translated by Ronald W. Sousa as *The Amazon: Land without History* (Oxford University Press, 2006). In *The Scramble for the Amazon and the "Lost Paradise" of Euclides da Cunha* (University of Chicago, 2013), Susanna B. Hecht sheds further light on that terrifying, radiantly narrated expedition. Three-quarters of a century later, another illustrious visitor who was somewhat less enraptured than horrified by the relentless vitality of the rainforest was Werner Herzog; *Conquest of the Useless: Reflections from the Making of "Fitzcarraldo"* (HarperCollins, 2009), translated from the German by Krishna Winston, is a record of his fraught stay in the region while filming the legendarily ambitious movie.

John Hemming's *Tree of Rivers: The Story of the Amazon* (Thames & Hudson, 2008) is a thoroughly engaging chronicle of a region so often misunderstood and of its peoples, rocked by centuries of brutal inroads. In *Naturalists in Paradise* (Thames & Hudson, 2015), Hemming follows the travels of

Henry Walter Bates, who spent eleven years in the Amazon in the mid-nineteenth century, as well as Alfred Russel Wallace and Richard Spruce, his contemporaries in tropical reconnaissance who collectively gathered countless samples and identified thousands of species during their time in Amazonia; Andrade's sprawling library included a copy of Bates's 1863 book, *The Naturalist on the River Amazons*, to which he makes a glancing reference during his visit to Puerto Sucre. In *Entangled Edens: Visions of the Amazon* (University of California, 2001), Candace Slater deftly navigates through the thicket of competing narratives around the region woven alternately by insiders and outsiders, not a few of which enchanted Andrade and clouded his eyes both prior to and during his trip.

Two notable novelists from Manaus, the riverine capital of the state of Amazonas, Milton Hatoum and Márcio Souza, have had several books published in English. To name one of each: Hatoum's *The Brothers* (Bloomsbury, 2002), translated by John Gledson, is the story of twins locked in a years-long battle for their mother's love, which also lends a window into the Lebanese Brazilian community in the Amazon in the early twentieth century; and Souza's *Mad Maria* (Avon, 1985), translated by Thomas Colchie, is a hyperbolic account of the construction of the hyperbolic Madeira-Mamoré railroad, a stupendously challenging feat that claimed thousands of lives and made Andrade feel a twinge of guilt about riding along the finished product.

While Andrade failed to make any meaningful connection with Indigenous peoples throughout his journey, readers will certainly benefit from lending an ear to Davi Kopenawa in *The Falling Sky: Words of a Yanomami Shaman* (Harvard University Press, 2013), written in collaboration with anthropologist Bruce Albert and translated by Nicholas Elliott and Alison Dundy. It presents the cosmology of the Yanomami people, who live at the far western reaches of the Brazilian Amazon, as well as Kopenawa's journey as a shaman and his vision of the deadly path the destruction of the forest has set us all on.

The Apprentice Tourist

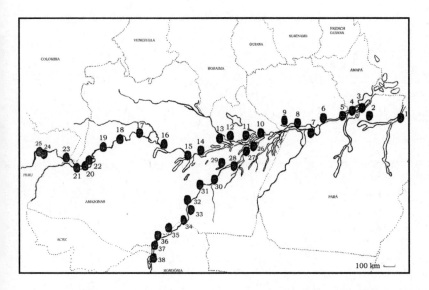

1 Belém (May 19–27, July 27–28, July 31–August 1)

2 Antônio Lemos (May 28)

3 Itamarati (May 29)

4 Gurupá (May 29, July 25)

5 Arumanduba (May 30, July 25)

6 Almeirim (May 30, July 25)

7 Santarém (May 31, July 24)

8 Barreira do Tapará (July 24)

9 Óbidos (June 1, July 23)

10 Parintins (June 2, July 23)

11 Itacoatiara (June 3, July 22)

12 Manaus (June 5–8, July 2, July 20–21)

13 Manacapuru (June 9, July 1)

14 Codajás (June 10, July 1)

15 Coari (June 11)

16 Tefé (June 12, June 30)

17 Fonte Boa (June 14, June 29)

18 Tonantins (June 15, June 28)

19 São Paulo de Olivença (June 16, June 28)

20 Esperança (June 18, June 27)

21 Remate de Males (June 18, June 27)

22 Leticia (June 19, June 26)

23 San Pablo (June 20, June 26)

24 Iquitos (June 22, June 25)

25 Nanay (June 23–24)

26 Borba (July 3, July 19)

27 Vista Alegre (July 4)

28 Manicoré (July 5)

29 Bom Futuro (July 6)

30 Três Casas (July 7, July 17)

31 Humaitá (July 7, July 16)

32 Calama (July 9)

33 Aliança (July 10)

34 Porto Velho (July 11, July 15)

35 Abunã (July 12)

36 Vila Murtinho (July 12)

37 Villa Bella (July 12)

38 Guajará-Mirim (July 12–14)

PREFACE

More of a warning than a preface, really. During this trip through Amazonia, quite determined to . . . to write a modernist book, probably more determined to write than to travel, I took many notes, as you'll all see. Quick notes, often telegraphic. A few stretched out more patiently tho, prompted by the rests imposed on our flat-bottomed steamer as it struggled against the river's rush. But almost all jotted down with no artistic airs, nothing meant to be polished or worked out, nor the slightest intention of revealing to others the land I traveled. And I never did really work it out. Sure, I made a few attempts. But I'd stop right at the start, not even sure why, just plain discontented. I'm sure I was displeased even back then by the personal nature of what I was jotting down. While I rejoiced and enjoyed my way up and down the Amazon, it's also true that I was sunk in myself all along that broad watery road.

Now I'm putting everything together here, just as it was in the notebooks and loose sheets, sometimes more written out, sometimes less. I only made a few unavoidable corrections as I copied it out. The whole thing wafts of modernism and has aged a good bit. But for the anti-traveler that I am, one who's always traveling wounded, fretful, incomplete, always casting myself as unwelcome in the strange places through which I pass, rereading these notes opens up feelings so immediate and intense that I find myself unable to destroy what I've preserved here. Ah, well . . .

SÃO PAULO
DECEMBER 30, 1943

SÃO PAULO, MAY 7, 1927

Departure from São Paulo. I bought an enormous bamboo cane for the trip, what a silly thing to do! It must've been some vague fear of Indians . . . I know full well there's nothing adventurous or dangerous about the trip we're about to take, but in addition to our logical faculties, each of us possesses a poetic mind as well. Half-remembered readings spurred me on more than the truth—savage tribes, alligators, bullet ants. And my saintly little soul imagined: cannon, revolver, cane, jackknife. And opted for the cane.

Well, in my eagerness to show just how calm I was, I kind of lost track of time, I forget the cane, remember the cane in the taxi, go back for the cane, and finally manage to make it to the station cane in hand. Just five minutes till the train leaves. I bid everyone farewell, seeming calm, feigning happiness. "Bon voyage," "Bring us back an alligator" . . . I hugged them all. And then there were still five minutes left again!

I'm not cut out for travel, for pity's sake! I'm smiling, but on the inside there's haunted, incest-colored regret. I go into my compartment, now it's too late, I've already set off, I can't regret anything now. A compact emptiness inside me. I sit in myself.

MAY 8

Rio de Janeiro. Lunch, as always on the days I arrive in Rio, with Manuel Bandeira.[1] I don't know, I find Rio an awfully ugly city, but people do say it's beautiful . . . The natural landscape is splendid, I know that, but the city, the urbanity of it, man's labors, man's suffering and glory, all that's thoroughly detestable. The most important thing to observe: the streets in the residential neighborhoods and the poor outskirts. The residential streets have a family-like air, an inside-your-house-in-the-morning air, not yet tidied up for the day, an indiscreet housecoaty air that isn't just an air, it's the plain truth. The people are still just as Debret[2] painted them, downright indiscreetly dressed in their doorways, out on the sidewalks. And the poverty—the workers in these neighborhoods have none of the architectural dignity that their condition warrants: the houses are garishly *ornate*, ramshackle, simultaneously unhygienic and ornate, putting on a show of happiness and celebration. Repugnant. At night I went with Luciano Gallet[3] out to the docks to meet a friend of ours who's arrived from Europe. Manuel Bandeira was there as well, enthusiastically awaiting a poet from Bahia, Godofredo Filho, s'posed to be quite good.

MAY 9

Rio. Lunch with Paulo Prado.[4] This is what happened: I get to the Copacabana Palace, eyes dazzled by the noon glare, I'm looking for Paulo in the whatsitcalled, the hall, I see someone waving to me sitting right next to the big window in the middle, it has to be him, I head that way. Once up close, yes it is Paulo Prado with Marinette, and . . . For heaven's sake! It's Graça Aranha, we're on the outs but it's a bit late for that now, I won't snub him, he doesn't deserve it, I wasn't the one who picked a fight.[5] He did, or at least pretended not to see me since I bawled him out in two articles for wanting to decide my life when I hadn't given him power of attorney. Paulo Prado gets up with an amiable air to set me at ease: "Have you met?" Graça Aranha gets up and ho-hos, half-deflated, "Oh, but of course!" I choke. And it all went well, we rebefriended each other, and the only disagreeable vestige of it all is that verb. Paulo Prado, when he's able to, tells me that the day before, after we'd arranged to meet, Graça Aranha announced that he'd be joining him for lunch that day. He felt obliged to say that I was invited but also found a way to add, knowing how I felt about the falling-out, that I had no hard feelings and he was sure I'd be cordial. But Graça said he'd think it over. That night he phoned Paulo to say he'd come to lunch and it was too late to consult me. I'm not sure about the "too late" part, Paulo Prado certainly didn't go to the trouble, knowing my feelings as he did. But it was a damned awkward surprise. I'd have come to lunch anyway, as long as I knew that Graça was willing to reconsider the act of blindness in which he pretended, unobtrusively it should be said, not to see me.

At night, hot as blazes! At Manuel Bandeira's house, taking the breeze in Santa Teresa. I meet Rodrigo Melo Franco de Andrade.[6] Manuel is still singing the praises of Godofredo Filho, assuring me that he writes the most splendid poetry and declaims it ever so well. And finally the poet starts in with the verses, eight, ten poems, there's no stopping him.

Suddenly I turn to Manuel and mutter: "But, Manuel! He can't declaim to save his life, and the poetry is just short of hateful . . ."

"Don't I know it! Back in Bahia, I swear I thought it was beautiful, but the second Godofredo started reciting in front of you all, I realized just how awful it is!"

MAY 10

Rio. Lunch with Manuel. Visit to see Ismael Nery's latest paintings.[7] Always very interesting, to be sure. He's always researching, cooking up things in his brain, brainy things, a bit harebrained if you ask me. More interesting than good. And so full of himself, honestly! Dinner and evening with Dantas and,

Good Lord, his wife! Finally, the gentleness of my friend and the damp rising off the lagoon.

DREAM

That night Machado de Assis[8] appeared to me in a dream, clean-shaven, and told me he was in hell.

"Poor soul . . ."

He chuckled a little and said: "But I'm in Dante's hell, the place where poets go. The only hardship is having to get along with the rest."

MAY 11

On board the *Pedro I*. I wasn't able to enjoy any of the sensations I'd planned to have upon my departure, since a gnawing worry distracted me completely. The porter they found to take my bags from the hotel to the docks, a little old man, turned up with one of those pushcarts, whatever they're called, with just two little fist-sized wheels in front. When I laid eyes on the cart I didn't like it one bit and my imagination saw the thousands of times those wheels would have to go round and round on their way from Lapa to the dock. And wouldn't you know I almost set off without my bags, which turned up at the last minute once the ship's luggage compartment had already been shut. What with all that going on I barely said goodbye to anyone and didn't notice how many travel companions were coming along for the ride. I knew we'd have a wild bunch from São Paulo, a real circus troupe, all great fun and up for anything. Well, when I got around to taking stock, everyone had flown the coop! It's just me, Dona Olívia and the two girls, Dolur and Mag.[9]

Dona Olívia, with that little smile of hers, says to me: "You must not be too pleased to be the only man along on the expedition . . ."

"If I knew I wouldn't have come, Dona Olívia."

Curt, sincere. She had nothing else to say. Neither did I. I was angry at her and the girls. She remembers to add that Washington Luís[10] telegraphed ahead to the governors of the states and to Peru. I don't say boo, but since it's very windy I excuse myself, go to my cabin, and swap my hat for a more appropriate travel cap. I looked in the mirror and managed to be a little easier.

Seen from the sea, Rio all lit up at night is hallucinatory. A fast-moving hallucination, to be quite explicit. I let myself go with it. The water moans, oily and leaden, lazily throwing back the frisky lights from the beaches. You can feel the festivities, they're throwing a grand romantic ball, suggested to me by the Ilha Fiscal.[11] An impossibly rich Croesus, the owner of the American sugar trust, why on earth sugar! is having the Queen of Sheba over at his castle in the Pyrenees. Telegrams sent out to buy all the lighted candelabras in the world and pick up all that jazz by authentic Negroes from the United States. Armies of servants run by with trays piled high with ice cream because it really is quite hot out. The Lady of the Camellias leans out the long low window over the waters and has fun spitting. Farther off, the Baron of Rothschild, the king of Belgium and a maharaja from who knows where tootling on brilliant silver whistles. Strolling by on the terraces, hard to make out, there's Paolo and Francesca, Paulo Prado, Tristão de Ataíde and Isolde, Wagner, Gaston Paris, Romeo and Juliet etc.,[12] gazing up at the stars, which are indeed in splendid health, eating ice cream because it really is quite hot out. Mad dancing in Largo do Machado, Lapa, Praça Onze.

. . . and then a murmuring frisson runs through the crowd packed along Avenida Rio Branco. Thousands of horses, white after the name of the avenue, bearing pages all clad in white satins and diamonds, emerge at an imperial gallop, wounding people, killing people, terrific cries of unhappiness, which are met by the songs of sirens upon sirens hidden behind the lights on the hills. And once the avenue is a pool of blood from end to end, here come elephants and camels bearing polished copper gongs striking, first the elephants which are the tallest, then the camels, then the lions, then the ferocious panthers roaring as they go, all at a pell-mell dash. And as soon as the panthers go by, bellies splashing through the blood running on the ground, seven hundred black slaves, tootling on whistles, bare naked with turbans of polished silver, come hauling, tugging on garlands of white camellias provided by the Lady of the Camellias, white Eulalias and white Magnolias,[13] a little white dock pushcart, which rolls along at a sublime velocity to bear the Queen of Sheba to her destination.

MAY 12

We don't stop at Vitória. I commence sweating buckets. So drowsy, not seasick but drowsy as all get-out! . . .

In the morning a butterfly moth showed up on board that must've been about ten and a half feet from wingtip to wingtip. It was oh so lovely, all in dark velvet with appliqués in Venetian lace. I was already acquainted with this sort, since a lady in my neighborhood keeps a pair in her garden. Even so, the apparition was received with general applause, because during the rushing around to try to catch the butterfly it always managed to find a way to introduce the passengers to one another, and that evening it put on a ball in the saloon.

Now we've been joined by yet another Swiss naturalist, Professor Hagmann who lives in Manaus, a moneybags called Humpity-Hump, the son of an Italian factory of São Paulo silks, a fellow wearing yesterday's clothes, the Adolescent in his undershorts winking at my companions, and, a bit ungainly, a grown man completely at home.

MAY 13

City of Salvador. Just terrific, I'm exhausted. But the devil of it is that there's no use saying "terrific," "wonderful morning," "delightful architectural invention," "beautiful girl." There's no use, it doesn't describe it. Those qualifiers only exist because man is a fundamentally envious being: you say that something is "wonderful" and he not only believes it but his imagination also magnifies whatever it was you felt. But if I could describe without tacking on qualifiers . . . Well, I wouldn't be me.

And since the night we set off, I've been trying not to introduce a certain someone. She's an American, a sugar-sweet summery girl and photogenic to boot. Pretending I don't know a word of English, I take photographs. It was enchanting to converse through eyes and gestures alone. I've never looked so lookingly in all my life and it truly is sublime. Perhaps as a result she pledged to me her eternal love, but was forced to stay in Bahia since I can't afford any entanglements.

MAY 14

Life on board, and I keep on sweating more and more. Schaeffer, the Swiss friend of John Graz,[14] introduces himself. Professor Hagmann is getting increasingly unbearable, bent on teaching us about Amazonia while only ever saying the most obvious things. Today, as he was telling us the meaning of the word *oca* in Tupi, Scales[15] asked naughtily, "So what does *dondoca*[16] mean?" But the professor didn't understand. He's too pure.

MACEIÓ

Still-bright nightfall, we stop by Maceió for a fat cat to get off. A boatman comes up singing "Meu barco é veleiro" (Mine's a Sailboat), a beautiful coco,[17] and sticks a harpoon into the *Pedro I*. Then they bring on so, so many mail bags, everyone on board is made amply aware that Alagoas is quite advanced on the score of epistolary literature.

DREAM

My dream went like this: I carefully wrote a speech in Tupi so that we might convey our greetings to all, once we were among the Indians. We met a tribe all assembled at the mouth of the Madeira, complete with a scrivener and a justice of the peace I could complain to if anyone were to mess with the Coffee Queen. Well, I recited my speech, which was a short one. But right from the start the Indians started exchanging looks and seeming like they were going to laugh. I soon saw that it was useless and that they were fixing to eat us all up. But that wasn't it: when I finished the speech, they all started shouting at me: "It's all wrong! It's all wrong!"

MAY 15

Recife and more Recife all day long—the pleasure was all mine, by the way.

Ascenso and Inojosa at the dock.[18] Boa Viagem Beach in the morning, chilled coconut water. Lunch at Leite, that inevitability of Recife, like the Butantan in São Paulo.[19] Ascenso's house all afternoon, him sing-saying verse after verse, completely oblivious to our restlessness or fatigue. Just guess where we had dinner? Leite. Outing to Boa Viagem under a sublime moon, those girls . . . Departure at midnight, having had such tremendous pleasure that not even Inojosa could dampen our spirits.

MAY 16

Never mistake another's cabin for your own without the resident's consent.

The mistake undone rather lamely, life on board goes on. What strange feelings I'm feeling . . . On land, even on vacation, I don't know . . . there's a sort of psychological predetermination that won't let you escape a single second from the notion, the feeling, the whatever-it-is of a struggle for life, or at least work. The sea cleans your being of that state of being. I realize that exercise does away with the drowsiness and this laziness that, while it aches a bit, is no heartache really. Round Cape São Roque. The sea of Ceará. Tomorrow we'll get to Fortaleza. It must be the recollection of the Padaria Espiritual[20] that sells me a Horatian cookie. "I like my Venuses easy and raring to go," I chewed away in the moonlight. I swallowed hard.

MAY 17

By morning, Fortaleza. We didn't get off, the stop was quite short. Lacemakers on board—those inevitabilities you already know you'll find in the city of Such-and-Such . . . Just imagine running across lacemakers from Ceará in Le Havre, how wonderful that would be! and surly French chauffeurs in Botucatu . . . Life on board. I'm still dripping sweat; I'll have some linen clothes made in Belém. But the drowsiness has been defeated. I don't know why, I remembered a story that my uncle Pio,[21] who's not my uncle, told me once. As a kid, he was playing with a little black boy, one of his father's slaves, the black boy did something or other, and Uncle Pio went: "Oh, you uppity little Negro, I'll tan your hide!"

"You try an' I'll run!"

"I'll run after you!"

"I'll git away between your legs!"

"I'll squat down!"

"I'd grab a rock an' hit you with it!"

"I'd dodge!"

"I'd grab a cane an' give you a caning!"

"Ain't got no cane!"

"I'd give you a switching!"

"Ain't got no switch!"

"Aw, I dunno! I'd grab whatever I could an' give you a whatevering!"

ON BOARD, MAY 18

Morning finds us in the middle of a canefield. So this is what they call the "wild green seas"[22] . . . It's a canefield and there's nothing wild about it. On the contrary, it's a meek servant, a Chalaça,[23] and *Pedro I* mounts on him and does as he sees fit. Frankly irritating. Cud-chewing a-courting cane-sucking while we're all impatient to see the mouth of the Amazon tomorrow. The mouth of the Amazon . . .

We were all atremble as we contemplated, from the pilot-house, nature's most famed monument. And I swear unto you that there is nothing so sublime in all the world. Seven kilometers out, the sea was already streaked with brown as the river water advanced. It was a tremendous gargantuan swath dappled with an amphitheater of forested islands so enormous that the littlest one was bigger than Portugal. The surging of the river and the clash of the waters formed tremendous eddies and swells and the waves broke seven meters high raining down foam foam foam pink with the Sun's dawning. And so the *Pedro I* forged on through a blooming shower. It forged on with difficulty, bucking and jumping, lurching over the flanks of baby whales and anacondas from the rainforest that had ventured out this far, led on by the freshwater mirage. As we drew closer, the islands, under the curtains of herons and storks that the wind drew back, were a catalogue of all the vegetable species, and in the fantastic hodgepodge of jequitibás perobas pine trees plane trees humbled by the vast bulk of the baobab we could make out the longed-for rubber trees dominating the tangle with the harvesters hanging from the most audacious branch tips on strips of raw leather to pluck the rubber fruits.[24] The scent of the pau rosa and the macacaporanga breathing from the resin of all the trunks was so inebriating that we swayed, nearly falling out into that big old world of furious water. What eloquence! The birds sang in flight and the din of the whistling ducks the flamingos the macaws the birds of paradise kept me from hearing the ship's bell calling for dinner. The Lady touched me on the arm and I started. I went with the others, leaving my wept-out thought on the magnificence of that hastily made landscape at whose heart there shone justprecisely like a glass eye the guaçu[25] wheel, the flooded island of Marajó.

On board the Pedro I,
May 18, 1927

MAY 18

Last day on board, a day made of nothings, with the precision of a Panama hat. The Arabian phonograph records of the Syrian from Belém, who winds up recommending the haberdashery he has there. It was he who reminded me of a Panama hat, since he wears one and sells lots of them, come from Iquitos. I don't know, I'd like to sum up my impressions of this coastal journey along Brazil's Northeast and North, and I can't quite do it, I'm a bit stunned, marveled, but I don't know . . . There's a sort of stubborn feeling of not-enoughness, of mottled motley colors, that absolutely wrecks the neat gray European I still have in me. For now, what I'm struck by is just how both nature and life in these places were cobbled together quite hastily, with far too much castroalves.[26] And I have this truly irresistible half notion that instead of using the Africa and India that it had within itself, Brazil has put them to waste, only using them to dress up its appearance, its skins, sambas, maracatus, outfits, colors, vocabularies, delicacies . . . And on the inside, it let itself remain that which, by virtue of climate, race, cooking, everything, it will never be able to be, will only ever be able to ape: Europe. We take pride in being the only great (great?) civilized country in the tropics . . . This is the flaw in us, this is what makes us impotent. We ought to think and feel like Indians, Chinese, folks from Benin, Java . . . Perhaps then we might be able to create a culture and civilization of our own. At least we'd be more us, I'm sure of that.

BELÉM, MAY 19

During the night, the *Pedro I* docked at Salinas to borrow a native pilot who could guide us through the treacherous mouth of the Amazon, and when we got up at the crack of dawn today we were already in it. What can I say of this river mouth, so literary, so awe-inspiring when regarded on a map? . . . The immenseness of the waters is so vast, the too-immense islands become far off and faint, and in the end you can't find anything to wonder at. The mouth of the Amazon is one of those grandeurs so grand that they overflow man's physiological capacity to perceive them. You can only monumentalize them mentally. All the retina puts into your consciousness is a big old world of muddy water and an unchanging scrub of forest on the faraway squinted-out islands. The Amazon is the final proof that monotony is one of the grandest elements of the sublime. It's an indisputable fact that Dante and the Amazon are equally monotonous. If you're ever to enjoy it a bit and make out the variety in these monotonies of the sublime, you've got to trap your sensations in tiny frames. Then you'll find the colorful sailboats charming and think the death of would-be beaus is just dandy, take hold of the tree-planted horizon that the refracted light cuts loose from the solid ground of the islands and put a hand on the Book of Job. The mouth of the Amazon is so gargantuan that its grandeur is a bluff. The Woolworth Building, the movie theaters in downtown Rio, and "I-Juca Pirama"[27] are far grander.

But when Belém commences, narrowing the broad horizon, beauty shows its face again. We got there before the rain and the heat was so fierce that the markets breathed out jerky-scented air. The sailboats sitting at the wharf at the Ver-o-Peso market shook their pink blue black sails, fanning themselves lazily. We were met ceremonially on the wharf by two government automobiles all ready for a flower parade.[28] A splendid bouquet for each of the poet's lady companions, and off we went. Then we reviewed all the flotsam and jetsam of the arrival. We reconvened only at night, for an excellent dinner. Belém had been inquiring about our tastes and kept a movie theater on the starboard corner of the hotel. We went to see William Fairbanks in *Do It Now*,[29] an awful flick. The night slept sound.

MOUTH OF THE AMAZON, MAY 19

And it is morningtime, a sublime morning. A few colorful sails, earth-colored water, some greens for a horizon. There's nothing to see! The mouth of the Amazon is only grand on the map; when you actually see it, everything is a size that you can't see. A few sails, earth-colored water, and some skimpy greens for a horizon. That's it. Arrival in Belém with official reception, Dionísio Bentes, mayor, etc., official automobiles, flowers for the women, and absolutely nothing of interest. Drowsy after lunch. Afternoon, "after the rain,"[30] we tried açaí. After dinner, once un-officialized, with nothing to do, we all went to the theater to see the important movie that all the papers and people were talking about, William Fairbanks in *Do It Now*—garbage.

BELÉM, MAY 20

Outings all day long, and I've already befriended everything.
I'm gleaming with happiness.

Belém is the greatest city in Polynesia. They called in a wave
of Malaysians, and in a cranny between the mango trees, Belém
do Pará was born. Funny, you always imagine that you live in
Brazil, but one gets a fantastic impression of being in Cairo. I
can't make out why . . . Mango trees, Cairo doesn't have mango
trees evaporating up from the streets . . . It doesn't have that
fellow out for a walk with a peccary on a leash . . . Much less
that individual who stepped across my eyes bright-and-early,
be still my heart! with the tail of his frock coat wagging behind
him . . . I jumped back and landed in the olden days. They say
that when my grandfather Leite Morais went to university to
teach law, he only ever dressed that way . . . Top hat and frock
coat and "Gentlemen, soonandsoforth, the defendant, upon
opening the umbrella of mitigating circumstances . . ." On one
occasion, getting a bit carried away, he famously shouted: "In
the square dance of the Law, the offense dances vis-à-vis with
the sentence!" I know who I took after . . .

At noon everyone went to lie down, and I only woke up for
my afternoon bath. It is fantastically hot here, altho I heard
from the locals that while Pará is really very hot, today is exceptionally so. Every five minutes I come out of the bath and
dry myself off, seven handkerchiefs, seventeen handkerchiefs,
twenty-seven handkerchiefs . . . Luckily I've brought three
dozen and will beat the washerwoman yet.

MAY 20

Peruvian consul, forty-five mil-réis. Sublime jaunt through the
market. We tasted so many things that, while each was only a
taste, we wound up stuffed. All generally tasty, much of it delicious, but you're left with a feeling of wildness, not just in your
mouth: in your being. I should have taken this trip when I was
much younger and much less experienced . . . Official visit and

intimate luncheon with the governor . . . did I say intimate? After the savories, the mayor got up with a coupe of champagne, a coupe! it'd been ages since I'd had champagne in a coupe, even with my rich pals in São Paulo . . . Well, he raised his coupe and made a speech welcoming Dona Olívia. And that's how it got started. From the minute that little man got up, I was on pins and needles, there was no way around it, I'd have to follow him! No sooner said than done: just as the mayor finished, Dona Olívia shot me a look with a little smile and with the tiniest gesture of expectation she conveyed that I was next. I'd never improvised anything in the world! A cloud darkened my eyes, I rose with a sense of doom, and then came an idea. Or something like it. I said that everything was so lovely, that we couldn't believe our eyes, and other identical bits of genuine nonsense, and then I let out the idea that we felt so at home (what hogwash!) that it seemed to us as if the state borders had been wiped away! I sat down as if I'd just been beaten with a stick. But the idea had . . . they'd liked it. That didn't change the fact that the champagne was sour, awful stuff. Then we visited the famous church of Nazaré and the splendid cathedral across from the archdiocese. And a spin around Souza in an automobile. I don't know, I take a voluptuous pleasure in nature, I luxuriate in it, but when I sit down to write a description it no longer holds any interest for me. There's something sexual in my enjoyment of landscapes and I don't know how to express it.

MAY 21

Morning: market, of course. Long visit to the Goeldi Museum, with a thorough tour. Library admirably well preserved by Dr. Rodolfo de Siqueira Rodrigues, one of those unsung heroes. I went to try on my linen clothes, and damned if I won't leave all of the clothes I brought from São Paulo at the hotel! At night, a ball at the Assembléia in honor of the travelers. I didn't go. It's amazing how worked up I've been, it's plain I still don't know how to travel, I enjoy myself altogether too much, I agree too much, I don't properly relish my own life. These notes in my diary are absurd summaries, only for personal use, jotted down in a little datebook given to me on the Lloyd Brasileiro,[31] which has only five lines per day. The literary stuff gets jotted down in another blank notebook, on letter paper, on the backs of bills, in the margins of newspapers, anything'll do. Jottings. Slapdash. Will have to see what can be made of all this in São Paulo.

MAY 22

Boat trip out to Chapéu Virado down the Maguari channel. River beaches, swimming in fresh water so close to the open ocean. Swarms of islands, schools of islets that come and go, vanishing here and there. This infinite variety of Amazonian heats. A breezy heat was beating down on the channel. Yesterday, after the rain, there came a heat so cool that the local women bundled up. And they say that out there, once we're in the heart of the immense river, there'll be mornings so damp we'll shiver with heat.

Jacumã: an oar with a blade that's almost round. In Pará they row at the bow, in Manaus, at the stern.

An urge to name things . . . I write the names down: Vila Felixana, My Haven, The Cenacle, Faith in God, Glad Harbor, Sweet Farm, Happy Rest, Pleasant Rest, Breezy Point, Chip's Café. Note the longing for a fresh breath of wind in some of the names: Breezy Point, Upended Hat . . .

What sumptuously colorful markings on the caladium leaves! And the swim was marvelous indeed.

Menu: snook. Duck with tucupi sauce. Suckling pig with farinha d'água. Bacuri compote, avocado cream, and murici ice cream, which tastes like Parmesan cheese with sugar.[32] And fruit, fruit.

*Chapéu Virado
Beach, Belém*

*Chapéu Virado
Beach. The Ford
balked. "Non
ducor, duco."*[33]

MAY 23

Belém thrills me more and more. The market was fantastically
welcoming today. Just the very sensation of mungunzá![34] . . .
Sitting on the ground in a white white blouse there was a black
black woman who lifted up to us her teeth her eyes the tube-
roses[35] on her turban, all white, and offered with outstretched
black arm a varnished black gourd from which wafted the
white steam from the white white mungunzá . . . I've enjoyed
myself beyond measure. Belém was made for me and I fit into it
like a hand in a glove.

In Belém the heat dilates one's skeleton and my body became exactly the same size as my soul.

MAY 23

Morning at the market. Bought a hammock, a Braque in its color combination.[36] Visit to newspapers, interview, a day lost to dull things.

MAY 24

Belém. Ah, the heat is mighty today, downright unbearable! "Let's git down south!," just like the aboio that a Pernambucan once sang to me . . .[37]

This morning we went to take the governor up on his lunch offer. And it was colossal! At the governor's mansion, they eat snook in tucupi sauce and the river-turtle meat melts away all the protocols and when the baritone taste of sapotilha swells on your tongue you simply forget the thousand virtues of homesickness and want nothing more: you go cross-eyed to make your happiness double and fall into the arms of the pleasantest mayor in the world, a fellow who's just as talkative as whiskey with coconut water.

MAY 24

Gubernatorial lunch again. Bentes's son is flirting with the two girls, and they accordingly flirt with him in tandem. Irritating, the feeling of being fooled around on. In the morning I went to Antônio do Rosário's to order pieces in tortoiseshell. Tea at the home of Mrs. Albuquerque, a little American lady. At night we went to the boi-bumbá[38] rehearsal at the Boi-Canário corral. The notes from this are in my papers on bumba meu boi.

MAY 25

Belém. Today the *Tucunaré* took us to lunch all the way out in Caripi. The Barcarena channel was dotted with sails. They say it's jam-packed with homes, but there's not one to be seen. Ever since the Paraguayan War, the caboclos[39] along this channel have hidden their houses away for fear of being called up to serve.[40] Once in a long while, a felled palm tree lying perpendicular to the shore will show up in a furrow in the foliage, dragging its mane in the water. They're used as landing docks— here be Indians.

It's still early for the Maracaguera primary school, and the ABCs haven't started up yet. Round about nine in all the houses in the neighborhood, the younguns start gathering up their lunches and their books, which double as ballast.

"Bye, Mama."

"God bless, João, you be careful!"

The youngun finds his big-bellied balance on the palm tree and jumps into the boat. It's a casquinho, as they call a canoe made out of a single small trunk, barely a boat at all, and off the youngun goes, rowing better than the folks at the Tietê Club, on his way to the Maracaguera primary school. Recess is for splashing around in the channel. Then it's back to the ABCs, and that way, later on, those fishermen can tot up the money they make off snooks and snappers, and can take the newspapers wrapping the farinha d'água from Belém and read about Lampião[41] and other specimens of Brazilian-born unruliness.

MAY 25

Wonderful outing to Caripi, what's the use of saying "wonderful!" if that doesn't begin to describe it, and I just can't. Lunch there. Swimming. Indian cattle, unfortunately, I can't help disliking . . . Sheep on the beach. I've seen a thousand European paintings with sheep in them, and I've seen my fair share of sheep at two or three farms in São Paulo. Ah, and I've seen sheep in agricultural shows. Then all of a sudden I see sheep on the beach, and there's no imagining how lovely it felt! I'd never even hypothesized a sheep on the beach! Ebb tide when we arrived at Caripi, the landing was a lark, everyone with their feet in the water. Except for the Coffee Queen (the name's sticking!) who was swept off by a sailor. Along came Bem-Bem with his guitar, and oh the way back around eleven at endless night, and all of us singing up on the steamer's roof . . . Among other stanzas were these, lustily sung:

> Yesterday at the church door,
> Before the mass was through,
> I said: "Look now, a saintly lady
> Stepping down into a pew!"

> The orange tree's leaves
> Look silver by night;
> Falling in love won't hurt you
> But parting sure might.

> The song that a man sings
> Won't ever be sung again.
> The love that a man scorns
> Can't ever be courted again.

MAY 26

Market, of course. Long visit to the Goeldi Museum, Marajó ceramics. Shopping. A farewell visit to the governor and to Mayor Crespo de Castro. Night with modernizing folk. I keep forgetting to mention Gastão Vieira, a doctor with literary intentions who's companioned himself to me since the first day, he admires me! Vague, terribly vague accounts of shamanism—these people simply take no interest!

The slime from the jaguar frog will make for happy hunting and fishing. First, you put ashes at the base of the tree where the frog lives (it stays up in the treetops), and if there are jaguar tracks in the ashes the next day, that's because the frog is really one of the ones that has the power to turn jaguar at night, an honest-to-goodness jaguaretê. Those are the ones you get the slime from.

The old Pará House of Mercy. Brother Caetano Brandão would gather the faithful at night and play the game of "I want you to go and come back and bring me such and such." "Two bricks," say. That's how the House of Mercy got built.

Fonte Boa, a place we'll be going through. Fonte Boa, Jaguaretê, Vila Bela . . . While the "scholars" on board say *pequeno almoço*, speaking in translation, the cabin boy only ever says *almoço pequeno*.[42] I do believe that there's an extremely Brazilian tendency to put the adjective after the noun. At least common people do. Note the difference between the Brazilian and Portuguese flavor in *o brilho inútil das estrelas* and *o inútil brilho das estrelas*.[43] That's not a good example.

Brazilian: *era um campo vasto* . . .
Portuguese: *era um vasto campo* . . .

MAY 27

Set out from Belém on the *São Salvador*, a kind of steamer called a vaticano.[44] The whole official cohort donoliviating[45] and bearing flowers. But my admirers are there too: Gastão Vieira, the two literary-minded young men from yesterday. I get this funny feeling, a hint of shame, a vague inner sense of infidelity when someone joins us on my account. On this trip, the only person who matters is the Coffee Queen, and that's just as it should be. The queen of my heart, for that matter, what a delight Dona Olívia is! We set sail. A nighttime stop in São Francisco dos Jacarés (Saint Francis of the Alligators). The mosquitoes had turned out in so many thousands that we struggled to move ahead and had to clear the way with our arms. The people down in third class apparently slice their way through the air with knives, blazing paths that, sadly, soon collapse on themselves. At times the mosquitoes formed such a compact mass that Mag and Dolur, both athletic sorts, were able to hang in the air—perhaps not as long as a minute, but a good forty seconds, swimming in the skeeters. In these "notes on my journey," as my grandfather Leite Morais called them, I often hesitate to recount certain things for fear I won't be believed.

MAY 28

Last night a summer storm came raging down. All hell broke loose! There was s'posed to be a wooding station on the bank that nobody could see, and the *São Salvador* came to a stop, groaning its heart out in the darkness, pleading for help, all tremendously sinister. But nobody came to the aid of the sinking vaticano, and here I swear I won't make a pun, my head's already full of them! Again and again, the heaving waves swept straight over the roof and we'd spend one minute, two minutes, holding our breath underwater. Children were carried off by the waves and their mothers lunged after them; only the captain, looking very pale, kept saying: "I'll stay! I'll go down with my ship!"—it was very touching. Eventually we began to make out a trail of light in the water, and out of nowhere there came the multiplication of the fishes, slow-moving and struggling to approach us, loaded up with firewood. I believe the Indians were afraid of us; they brought as much firewood as we needed, but simply couldn't be convinced to come up on board so we could introduce them to the chicken we'd brought solely for that purpose.[46] So we gave up and the steamer moved on.

Fresh, cool morning. A gang of parrots greets us, bidding us good morning in Abanheenga.[47] Now and yonder, a heron. The Straits of Breves. Life on board. The silly little things that make the trip sublime: for example, a river dolphin playing in the water. A river dolphin playing in the water! just think of that!

Stunning landscapes. Sublime starry night. We stop at the town of Antônio Lemos.

MAY 29

Morning finds us at a wooding station. Still in the straits. Riverside cemetery. Finally out on the Amazon itself. We stop at Itamarati, a beautiful little outpost, home to the first truly scarlet ibis I've ever laid eyes on. Stilt platforms dripping with flowers, "hanging gardens" in places where one never knows how high next year's floods will rise. Dogs that've never known what it is to run, perched up on top of the platforms. We steam along, hugging the bank. The children from the near-always invisible riverside homes paddle out in their little boats—each of them has one—to catch the steamer's wake and have the chance to ride some lively waters. The hoatzins give themselves away as they go by, flying decently enough and lifting their tails as they land with a thud—they seem to weigh a ton. And the mosquitoes here are the worst yet . . . Everyone seems to feel obliged to "tell" us what things are, I can't take it anymore! They've already shown me the açaí palm a thousand times, pointed out the hoatzins a hundred times, explained that that's the river dolphin playing in the water, for pinecones' sake! Round around afternoon, we passed the Xingu River on our port side. Grub on board (at least ours, which is special) is always delicious. There's too much dancing, and what with no want of heat and great want of love, it's getting tiresome. Gurupá, a falling-apart frontier outpost. The fort. The church.

I'll describe this morning's firewood stop: they carry a thousand logs into the ship's belly to make two mil-réis.

MAY 30

Morning finds us at the famous Arumanduba Farm, property of the greatest millionaire in Amazonia, Senator José Júlio de

Andrade.[48] The man's fame has preceded him and pursued us ever since our arrival in Belém: a sort of strongman with two hundred, three hundred henchmen, "made of money." It's true we didn't talk about him with "official" people, but the lump sum of what I heard is that the man's no good. Everyone, poor folks, middling-class types, it's clear, harbor something between dread and detestation of the man. But this, it's clear, is a genuine . . . eruption of class. It was a short stop, we didn't see anything. Passed the tumbledown town of Almeirim on our starboard side. Clouding over. We're chased down and overtaken by a Lloyd steamer, the *Duque de Caxias*. Rumors of Tarsila and Osvaldo on board, only rumors.[49]

A remarkable, painfully human case of folk etymology: in the distance we spotted the Serra da Velha Pobre [Poor Old Lady Mountains], which had actually been dubbed the Serra da Velha Nobre [Lordly Old Lady Mountains] after an honest-to-goodness aristocrat, very old indeed, who lived around there god knows when. But the locals didn't take to pecking orders apart from those of poverty . . . And so 'twas that the Lordly Old Lady became the Poor Old Lady.

I saw cattle wintering on a maromba, a sort of oversize platform where heavy livestock can live while the river's high. A melancholy sense of insufficiency, of an error at the root of things.

In the Amazon, they don't cut dogs' tails; that way they can balance on top of an estiva. Estiva: generally a felled açaí palm serving as a pontoon bridge at a port. What passes for a port around here is sometimes little more than a crevice in the jungle and a halfway smooth dirt slope, dissolving into the muddy river water.

MAY 31

Life on board. Delightful to stretch out in these comfortable chairs on the deck at the bow and let yourself exist almost completely through sight, no ponderation whatsoever, staring at the jungle, which is so close it often scrapes the ship. First alligator spotted, tremendous to-do. Egrets. As the afternoon announced itself, we arrived at Santarém, with its odd Venetian air thanks to the hotel anchored at the port with its facade slipping down into the water, and with Gothic windows! The Venetians speak our tongue quite well and are all a deep, even shade of Tapuio brown.[50] We were welcomed very cordially by the doge, who showed us the city, which ends allofasudden. The clock at City Hall was stopped, and this allowed us to understand Santarém as it was thirty years ago. We became wonderfully inclined in the city's favor, and the nuns put on a little children's parade, with an extremely pleasant breeze coming off the flags.

The shrewdness of poverty . . . At the mouth of the Tapajós I saw boats with strange sails, which were the hammocks in which the fishermen slept, strung up to catch the wind. By night, hammock; by day, sail.

To be or not to be Venice. Here you have the ogive windows of Santarém.

THE CASE OF THE POTBELLY

This is one of the most profoundly Venetian patriotic deeds of which I have ever heard. Some time ago, an American committee was going round the Amazon, studying the problem of the rubber trade and fixing to find a site with all the necessary conditions, health concerns included, where the Americans might set up shop. They went here and there, took a shine to Santarém and surroundings, and, to show in their report just how promising the place was, they started photographing all the able-bodied Venetians. Now, round here there lived a young family in which the wife and two children were simply the finest expressions of local able-bodied beauty; word has it the little ones were dazzlingly hale. And they had achieved a singular miracle: they weren't potbellied. The husband very patriotically agreed that his folk could be photographed, but he himself was suffering from malaria. So what'd he do: as the Americans set up his wife and two little ones outside their home to take their picture, the man went in and wrapped himself all up in the hammock, not even the tip of his nose out, so he wouldn't show up in the photograph. But from that day on the man started getting down in the mouth, a gloom that everybody tried their best to shake but nobody could. The thing was, deep down he was fretting and fretting that in spite of all the care he'd taken to hide himself in the hammock, the photograph might have gotten him too. Then the Americans would forever reject Amazonia and the land wouldn't get rich, and all because of his malarial skin and bones. Folks consoled him, told him that was all nonsense, but it proved impossible to shake the patriot's sorrow; he got sadder and sadder, stopped eating out of sadness, and one Wednesday, he up and died of sadness. I'm just telling the story for its own sake, I should say, not to hold up this sublime patriot as an example for Brazilians. I mean, if all the Brazilians unworthy of this vast country were to patriotically die . . .

JUNE 1

Around midnight last night, we stopped at Tapará Farm so that twenty beef cattle could be loaded on. What an inhumane sight! Here's how they do it: A man comes running along a kind of corridor of planks leading out to a terrace by the water—the lights of the ship grant he's wearing one last shred of ragged trousers. After him comes a bucking hopping mad ox. Then a troupe of half-naked Tapuios with admirable physiques pops up on the terrace, bodies glistening in the fortuitous drizzle, in a tremendous bit of theater. The group dances a whole lively mazurka of halloos behind the ox: *"eeeh, boi!"* That's all you hear, *"eeeh, boi,"* *"eeeh, boi!"* The man in front runs up to the edge of the planks and tosses the ox's rope over to the ship. The rope flies into the darkness, but on board the infallible worker who never misses a catch grabs it and bellows: "Go!" Then the Tapuios' racket howls into joyous hysteria that puts a fine point on the ox's terror. The poor animal throws itself into the water and comes swimming alongside the ship. The man with the rope pulls the ox along, gets it in place, gets the crane loop around the critter's horns, and—"Slow, now!"— lets it know what's coming. And the little saint, hands crossed over its chest, eyes full of unbearable terror, is born from the waters like the day and gently rises up and up, its thoughts on God. But then a diabolical arm interrupts the ascension, grabs the critter by the tail, and yanks it over to the ship. The crane goes down a bit and the ox is grabbed any old which way and pulled onto the lower deck, where it's soon sleeping among the hammocks in third class.

A full day. Pirarucu at lunch, excellent. Before the rain, there came a heat so fertile that we were able, using an ordinary magnifying glass, to observe one another's beards growing. I believe it is because of the heat that the Indians in this region have prodigious beards, which they carry around in their laps, done in extraordinarily complicated braids. And custom demands that the alligators show themselves on the first of June in the flooded forests by the river so that the tourists may contemplate them gleefully. We spotted lots of them, floating in the water.

Then Óbidos. Met by the superintendent, at whose house I tried a very well-made taperebá liqueur. Delicious. With less sugar it'd be magnificent. Visit to the traditional fort, with its tame cannons. Óbidos has many streamers and a bandstand thatched with palm fronds in front of the church. This is how the locals show the tourists that the town is very festive. If you ask hopefully if there are any festivities to attend, willing to wait and see them, the Obidenses respond in unison that they happened just the day before, closing out the month in honor of the Virgin Mary. This keeps expenses down while still spreading the word about how terrifically festive the town of Óbidos is. A shoal of jaraquis was going by, the water bubbling with them and the fishermen slaving away. "If you eat jaraqui, you'll never leave," goes the saying around here. Out of spite, the cook presented us with a "Portuguese-style" tucunaré for dinner. I can safely say that this other fish was toothsome in its own right, and that Óbidos found its place in me.

JUNE 2

Life on board. Afternoon in Parintins with the chatty mayor. He offered us a book about the town—so many books already, so many reports! . . . Quite a peculiar crucifix at the church. I give unto you the rules of the Apostleship of Prayer:

1. Renounce dances altogether.
2. Renounce masks and costumes.
3. Take no part in private festivities (prayer at private residences is not permitted by the vicar).
4. Ladies must renounce the excesses of fashion, wearing neither low-cut garments nor cutting their hair.
5. At church and in processions, ladies must always wear veils.

6. At mass and at processions, ladies must not carry fans.
7. Attend confessions and communions as often as possible.

In Parintins. The only person who didn't pop out of a door or window to see us was the girl who died this very day, stabbed to death by her love. At night, drifting on the water, we heard the crying of the howler monkeys. It's a human lament, a ghastly one, which left us utterly deflated.

DUCK-BLIND STEER

This is what they call a trained steer that sidles nonchalantly up to the ducks and stops right by them. Then the hunter, who's been hiding behind the duck-blind steer, takes his shot.

JUNE 3

Deep in the small hours. A dead alligator floating belly-up with its feet sticking straight into the air. More than seven hundred (the number was provided to me) more than two hundred egrets take flight from the light green grass. At lunch, tambaqui: an excellent fish, tremendously delicate. And turtle stuffed with itself, a masterpiece. Around two o'clock we'll dock at Itacoatiara, the first city in the state of Amazonas. Seen in dreams. It's the most beautiful city in the world, you've got to see it to believe it. It has seven hundred triangular palaces made of very soft, furry granite, each with a single door of red marble. The streets are all liquid, and the general mode of transportation is the manatee—for women, the river dolphin. I soon spotted a bunch of gorgeous girls dressed in scarlet, riding on river dolphins that bore them swiftly to the palaces, where they invited me into chilled halls with gold and silver hammocks for a swaying rest. There was just one hammock, and we two fell into it easily. We made love. Then we went to visit the public monuments, where we made love once again because all the bureaucrats were busy and didn't even spare us a look. The streets weren't rightly named after people. There was My Dear Street, Vamp Street, Coffee Queen Street, Young Ladies' Street, Steely Profile Street, Carnival Street, Against the Apostleship of Prayer Street. And all of the gorgeous girls let me cut their hair quite readily. I cut and cut and cut away, awash in a sea of hair, which was delightful if a tad hot. And that's when I was woken up.

Pardon and so on but there was somebody who had to speak with me. Three o'clock. I heard a louder than usual hubbub as I applied a bit of cold water to my person. Lights through the cabin roof, ah! Itacoatiara. And the regional police captain had come as a representative of the governor of the state of Amazonas and the mayor of Manaus, plus the mayor of Itacoatiara (indisposed) to welcome Dona Olívia and company to the state. Well.

JUNE 4

What with being woken up and all I never got back to sleep, but I had a marvelous night to make up for it. For that matter, I've noticed and am starting to get accustomed to the fact that folks on board will do anything at any time. Whenever the heat pushes you out of the cabin in the middle of the night, you'll find all sorts of people, pajamas, even women, strolling on their own or deep in conversation. Sometimes we wake up the barman.

And it was a wonderfully entertaining day thanks to the enchantments of the riverbanks, more populated than ever, we're getting closer to Manaus. The steamboat stops so they can cut swamp grass to feed the cattle that are on board to feed us. Then all of a sudden the field of swamp grass parts to reveal a little boat. Three women are in it, but only the old woman comes on board the steamer. One of the young women had a simply sublime figure, just gorgeous, what a body! . . . And on top of everything she was the one rowing, her body straining out of her tight white muslin dress. Why I called the fabric *muslin* I don't know, it must be a class thing. We made a hullabaloo over the girl, but she didn't look at us even then, not even a look! What's really commendable in these Indian women from the Amazonian lower classes is their discreet, albeit graceful elegance when nude—so different from civilized women![51] In Greece, in the Renaissance, at least as far as the paintings and sculptures tell it, women still looked all right when they were naked, but for a good while now . . . they can get naked all right, but they get this gawky, discombobulated, housecoaty air about them. It's horrible. I've never seen a contemporary bourgeois woman who didn't get all housecoaty when she undressed. Of course I'm speaking purely in terms of beauty, because by and large nudes have always been quite enjoyable company. But the steamer stopped again. It was a wooding station, but we weren't in need of wood. We're taking our time so we can get to Manaus in the morning, and that way the reception will be all the prettier.

THE PROBLEM OF THE LITTLE FAUCET

Since we'd stopped at the wooding station, we went to see the famous liana, the one that the Indian girl from that beautiful story "The Village of the Moon," having gone around doing a few unmentionable things with her brother, used to climb up to the sky and become the moon.[52] The vine is still going strong in its venerable old age. It's shrunk over the years, as is only natural, its trunk all wrinkled, the roots so colossal that seventy of us were able to bivouac in the shadow of a single one. Truth be told it's not exactly a liana vine, as the Indians so imprecisely put it, but an apuí tree, that's what it is. The tree it grabbed onto to make its way up into the sky was a formidable balata, the biggest in the world—which, evidently, was choked to death by the strangler. One can still get quite a good sense for the hulking size of the balata, because while it rotted and disappeared bit by bit and was carried away by ants, the space where it stood was left inside the apuí tree. The hollow, as best we could tell, is about seventy meters across and seven hundred high. This generous, providential bosom became home to the hives of all sorts of Brazilian bees, from guarupus and bijuris to mandassaias and tubunas. It is extraordinary, doubtless one of the most scrumptious spectacles in the world. Foreigners have come all the way from the other side of the globe to get a look at it. From seven leagues away you can hear the buzzing, as mellow and monotonous as electric lighting. Up close it's a veritable symphony, with honey trickling down the roots and shellacking the ground. As you'll surely know, the Brazilian government had the bright idea to install, below the massive hollow-cum-hive, a tremendous sheet of steel with a little faucet on it. That way, whoever wants to can go over, turn on the little faucet, and fill up with all the honey he needs. Or even all the honey he doesn't need, which is a real shame. But in any case, it seems that the issue of hunger has been solved for us. A procession leads up to the Government's little faucet: local rubber tappers, Muras, Parintintins,[53] Taulipangs from the Guyanas, Americans, Syrian peddlers, Argentine traders, Paroaras,[54] plenty of Canadians, the language of Goethe, a colorful hodgepodge of races. The Canadians and the English even formed a Swiss union to help our Government build a summer hotel a short distance from the apuí tree, with floors upon floors and every comfort imaginable. The Government waived taxes and customs obligations for all the material brought in for construction: reinforced concrete, works of art, perfumes, seventy thousand yards of silk, rotary printing presses, Italian hats, footwear, typewriters, radios, ladies' winter furs, precious stones, slightly immoral and thoroughly French novels, lace, etc. And indeed there was so much interest that they soon granted the union seven hundred square leagues of land in the middle of a rubber tree plantation, with permission to harvest it all: rubber, nuts, women, livestock.

As is customary, we tried the "apuí honey," as people call it around there. It is quite tasty, albeit a fair bit dirty, since it comes out mixed with lots of pollen. This is the case because Brazilian bees remain deeply ignorant of the new techniques in hive architecture introduced by *Apis mellifica*. They mix it all together, the honeycombs with the eggs, the wax with the pollen—it's a terrible shambles in there. If you poke around for some honey, you'll come up dry, but you'll find pollen all right. Not even the bees themselves know what they're doing. Many, as they look for honey in the hive that they built themselves, discover that they don't know where it is, spend their whole lives looking for it, and ultimately starve to death. But I'm talking about ordinary hives, of course, which are all over the place in Brazil. You don't see that kind of mess with the apuí honey, thanks to the Government's little faucet. You open it up, and bingo: more honey than you know what to do with. People even say that lately the honey was running dry, all because the bees themselves up and stopped working. Since they're not strong enough to open faucets on their own, they hang around the lip of the blessed thing, waiting for a tourist to come over, open the tap, and let the honey out. No good can come of a hive like that.

JUNE 5

After yet another nighttime storm, we arrive in Manaus with the sun high in the sky. Official reception, we're introduced to seven hundred and seventy-seven people, there's a cavalcade (how funny it is, being an important figure in an official procession), then off to the Rio Negro Palace, with an official reception straightaway by the acting governor, a real charmer. Then off to Hermosina Farm, where we had a colossal lunch, absolutely colossal. After we come back, I take advantage of twilight to visit the red-light district. Later the colonel, chief of police, took us to the neighborhood of Cachoeirinha to visit the fair at the Church of the Poor Devil, where the festivities were just like ours back home—a grease pole, auction, going once, going twice . . . Calm, respectable sleep.

Tonight I tried soursop ice cream. Strange . . . soursop tastes like soursop, there's no getting around that, but it's not exactly an independent flavor. Rather, it's an image, a metaphor, a hasty synthesis. It's the very image of all of those herbs and fruits used for seasoning that, once overdone, make you heartily sick of them. Not bad exactly, but irritating. For that matter, the guaraná around here, or at least what I tried, has an empty taste—once you've drunk it down, it leaves you where you started.

JUNE 6

Morning: streetcar ride, official procession over to the brewery. Official afternoon as well, hospital, orphanage, Ângelo Guido exhibition, we didn't buy anything. Free night for me, with Raimundo Morais, Da Costa e Silva, and others, all averse to any brand of "futurism"[55] but who felt it was their collegial duty to visit me. Extremely pleasant, great conversation, very little literature, lots of Amazonas and high spirits, the result being that they brought me back on board at three in the morning. They gave me the gently mocking little piece they published on the occasion of my futurist visit. It's not exactly funny, tho.

Acariquara is a tremendously odd sort of tree, s'posed to be stronger than iron, with elongated holes running up and down it.

Banzeiro is what they call the rippling of the waters when a ship goes by and leaves its wake, disturbing the river's calm. It's so hot out! hotter than Belém even.

Festa da Moça Nova, a puberty rite among the Ticunas. A month beforehand, they shut the pubescent girl up in a house, then they get her drunk on caiçuma till she's rolling on the ground. Men with animal masks dancing around her. The women of the tribe come up and start pulling out her hair until it's completely gone. Not a single strand escapes. Anywhere on her body.[56] Well, who had the bright idea to talk about a thing like that near the young ladies—they got all in a tizzy. And then I'm left with them!

Chula: around here, they use the word *chula* for a sort of song, generally a comic one and just shy of up-tempo, an allegro co-modo. Here's a stanza of the chula "Cachaça," which has no refrain, from the time when Manaus banned shops from selling booze on Saturday nights:

> If I should die, lay down on my casket
> The purest stuff in the largest cask
> Run the pipe to my lips, and by and by
> Before you know, I'll drain that cask dry

Here's the refrain of another one, quite a fluvial ditty:

> Turn larboard, starboard, bow, and stern
> Turn this way and that
> Can't say if it's good, can't say if it's not
> Turn that thing around, now!

Casting the net

At Amaniúm Lake,
outside Manaus

JUNE 7

Outing in two official boats down the Careiro, bad weather.
We set off from the Negro and headed down through Catalão.
Whole day out. We went to Lake "Amaniúm," not sure I heard
that name right, I have to ask. But what a sublime thing, that
lake, surrounded on all sides by a colossal wall of forest, calm,
an enchanted calm, in which noises, animals' cries, ring out
and waste away. Solitude that's pure and free, not a bit melancholy. There were the water lilies, with uapés[57] and herons
perched on their leaves. We came back at dusk. The two boats
racing each other. At night, nothing to do, abandoned by the
locals who wanted us to rest up, we went to the movie theater.
They were showing, for pity's sake! they were showing, with
great fanfare, William Fairbanks in *Do It Now.*

———

Cabroeira:[58] a dance done by the blacks in Bahia.

The timber raft, up to five thousand logs in some cases, head-ing down to Manaus since May. Some of them go all the way to the Straits of Breves, where they're broken up so the logs can be sent off to furrin parts, the United States mostly. They're broad drifting islands that whole families camp on for months, building their homes there, bringing on cows, pigs, chickens, and pets—trained parrots, dogs, favorite caladiums—all mak-ing a life together as they drift down this big old world of water. Sometimes the raft is hit by a chance current, rams into some bank, a hard shore, a river neck, a flooded forest, and all comes tumbling down, it's the end. Everything comes to pieces, the logs scatter, some move on, others don't. But in general when the waters are high, they flow from the banks to the cen-ter of the river—and so the rafts, given unto themselves, make it all the way down. But always with a questioning air, will they arrive? will they not? Nobody knows and nobody can know, it's dumb luck.

VICTORIA AMAZONICA[59]

At times the water of the Amazon retreats behind the embaúba trees, and in the yonders of silence it pools into lagoons so se-rene that even the cries of the uapés sink below the surface. Well, it is in these lagoons that the water lilies live, calmly, ever so calm, fulfilling their flowery fate.

Like balls of rubber sap, all curled up and pricklyful, the young leaves thrust themselves up from the still mirror, but the adult ones who know better open up a round plate, rest on the water, and hide the wickedness of their thorns down in it.

When the time's ripe, the bud bursts up out of the water too, a thorny little hedgehog that not even a bug will land on. And so it grows and plumps, waiting for the morning of its flow-ering.

At long last one sunup the water-lily bud splits its spines, shivers open, and the vast flower gets to whitening the calm of the lagoon. Petals petals free themselves white white scads upon scads, in a short span of morning the vast flower opens up a world of white white petals, white petals, and it aromas the indolent air.

A gentle entrancing smell sways, a smell that calls out, dizzying the strongest senses. So row, row over and take the flower. The thornful petals take a furious bite and blood trickles from your hand. The stem can't be held, it's all thorns too, there's nothing for it but to cut, and as the flower floats on the water, lift it up by its pure petals, ruining the whole thing a bit.

Then strip the thorns from the stem and, at your ease, smell the flower. But that delicate aroma which enchanted lightly from afar is slippery up close, nauseating, an awful smell . . .

And then the water lily gets to pinkening all over. It pinks, pinks, gets all rosy, calling over from far off with that nice scent, prettier all the time. That's how it is. It lives a whole day, always changing color. From rosy it goes bloodred, and round around nightfall, over-old, it softens its necklaces of purple petals.

In all these colors, the water lily, the great flower, is the most perfect flower in the world, the loveliest and the noblest, sublime. It is the supreme form of the image of the flower (that was once the idea of Flower).

Night falling, the purple water lily is all purple, almost on the point of closing again and dying, when the old lady gives one last heave and opens up the petals at her center, still closed, closed up tight since they were all in the bud. Well, she opens, and there from the nuptial heart of the great flower, still stunned by the breathing air, emerges a scurryflurrying pollen-crusted nasty repulsive flock of tea-colored beetles.

This, the last contradiction of the sublime flower . . .

The nasties set off to buzzbuzz their way into the world, an ominous stain on the calm of the sleeping lagoon. And in the vast night, the great flower of the Amazon, lovelier than the rose or the lotus, draws to a close its flowery fate.

JUNE 8

Morning visit to the market in Manaus, far less interesting and less lavish than Belém's. We tried tucumã coconuts, downright awful. At lunch we tried matrinxã, which I thought was one of the best fish in the Amazon. Visit to the rubber processing plant and the commercial association, remind me why again? Ah, I forgot to say: pupunha fruit with molasses is a real treat too. We left Manaus at five in the afternoon, with all the administrative apparatus of the state on the dock and a band to see us off. Life on board. This thing of being the only man on a trip with women can get very very masculine, but.

THE TRIBE OF THE PACAÁS NOVOS[60]

Yesterday, when we were out on the launch, we happened to visit the tribe of the Pacaás Novos, a people of peculiar ways and customs. As soon as we got within a quarter of a league of them, there commenced a stink that moved us so disagreeably and was so repulsive that I was able to overcome it only with great effort and arrive at their hutment. Unfortunately my lady traveling companions gave up on seeing it, which meant that they could not bear witness to all that I was then able to admire. The architectural structure of the settlement comprised the big house and a dozen small houses, quite similar to those made of adobe and thatch in the south. When I arrived, a couple of kids playing along the trail sent up the alarm in a strange way, without a single cry. They hopped up and down, moving their little legs in the air with great speed and a variety of leggy gestures. Then they ran away, going to hide their utter nakedness in their little hovels. I imagined that this was fear of white folk, but no, it wasn't: when I came up to the beaten-earth clearing, a sort of square surrounded by constructions, they came out of their houses and surrounded me without the slightest ceremony, a whole crowd of men and women dressed in the most extraordinary way. The kids then began to attack me, giving me an unimaginable variety of kicks. What's more, they moved the toes on their feet in a prodigiously nimble way. Given my work as a piano teacher, I found myself observing principally the movement of the fourth toe, which was astounding! I believe that not even one percent of the pianists in São Paulo (which, as we know, number in the millions) can twiddle away with such tremendous digital independence. I arranged for, well, no, what happened was an old skinny Indian as ugly as a vast Amazonian sunny day came over saying that he was an interpreter and that he charged seven mil-réis for the hour. I accepted, and he told me that with those gestures, the kids were asking me for presents, over and over again . . .

Back to the grown-ups. Their dress, if one might call it that, was as follows: They were entirely nude, with their voluminous abdomens painted with two crescents of urucum, one on each side, all velveted because of a very fine flour-like face powder sprinkled on top, which the Pacáas Novos extract from corn aged for this purpose. Around their necks, however, a thick cord woven of spotted palm held up a fine cloth made of curauá, richly decorated with little ribbons of canarana fiber and extraordinarily delicate lace made of filaments of munguba. With this, they fashioned a sort of petticoat, which instead of covering their shoulders and falling over the rest of their bodies, rose into the air, held up by oscillating fins harvested from fish. These petticoats, raised to the sky, covered the Indians' heads completely, with only a minuscule orifice in front, at the part more or less corresponding to the eyes, allowing them to see out. Through this orifice, I was able to perceive that, in addition to the petticoat, the Indians had wrapped their heads in a filthy cloth, the nature of which I was unable to discern, which also had convenient openings at eye level. Beyond this strange garb, the Pacáas Novos' arms and hands were completely clothed with sleeves of jaguar pelts, or anteater or otter hide, or maned wolfskin, etc., cut in a fashion that bore some resemblance, although I may be embellishing it a tad, to the famous leg-o'-mutton sleeves that the white ladies of old used to wear.

I was dumbfounded, contemplating said garb, and then, because of the sun, I felt a tickle in my nose, which was bedeviled

by the prevailing smell, and I let out a little daisy chain of
sneezes, what on earth possessed me! The women fled behind
the houses, making great gestures with their legs that I later
found to be gestures of intense reproach. The men, however,
and the kidlings began moving their shoulders and bellies so
expressively that I did not need the interpreter to realize they
were laughing. But not a sound could be heard. They laughed
with their shoulders, bellies, and legs. For that matter, the gestures they made, especially with their legs and their lively
toes, were so expressive in their kicks and contortions, let me
repeat, they were of such an inexhaustible variety that I, with
my extensive knowledge of languages, who speak German,
English, and Russian with great aplomb and have a reasonable
mastery of French, Tupi, Portuguese, and other tongues besides, soon became familiarized with the language of the Pacaás and understood much of what they were thinking and
communicating.

Then the interpreter commenced explaining the customs of
the Pacaás. He spoke very quietly, with his mouth disagreeably
up against my ear, but even so the Indians seemed to only
barely tolerate our muttered exchange. You see, the Pacaás
Novos are quite different from us. For them, the sound and the
gift of speech are terribly immoral and formidably sensuous.
Their private parts and the not-showable areas of their bodies
are not the ones we all consider to be so. When they feel it is
their business to do their business, they do it wherever they
please and in front of whoever may be there, even on the feet or
legs of others, without the slightest hesitation, as naturally as
our country folk hawk and spit. But a sneeze, for example, or
any sound from the mouth or nose–those noises should be let
out only when one is by oneself, in their estimation. The result
being that when a Pacaá feels a sneeze coming, he sets off running, scampers into a solitary patch of forest, sticks his face
into the leafiest topsoil he can find, and sneezes in private, very
politely. They consider the nose and ears to be the most shameful parts of the body, not to be shown to anyone, not even one's
parents, only to be seen between man and wife in their most
intimate moments. Listening, for them, is what we call a mortal

sin. Speaking, for them, is the ultimate sexual act. While acts of procreation may occur at any time and any place, in front of everyone, this does not happen frequently, fortunately for me, since the gestures that arouse love stem solely from phonation. They harbor an institution quite similar to our sacrament of matrimony, and when a man falls in love with a woman, the two of them start a-whistling with the most delicate subtlety, this being their courtship. One fine day, the beau comes up to his sweetheart's father's house and says that he's come to ask for her voice. If the father consents, following a bacororô[61] that lasts between seven and seventy days, according to the groom's means, all in silence and involving many a thing that we would find reprehensible, the new couple go into their home and, behind closed doors, all the nooks and crannies caulked with the plumage of fine feathered friends, they get to talking with abandon. The next day, when the sun's just about in the middle of the sky, the parents of the bride, just the two of them, come up to the couple's door and make their arrival known by shaking the walls. Then if the new bride puts her lips to a cranny in the adobe and lets out a whistle, the marriage is consummated. If not, they eat the husband.

Speaking of which, the act of eating is also considered terribly reprehensible, as it requires one to show one's mouth. So behind their homes the Pacaás build private little rooms in tucked-away places where they always keep stores of powdered corn, bananas, and fish meal, their habitual diet. When one of the Indians in a family feels hungry, he keeps it to himself, makes sure nobody is watching, and makes himself scarce. Then he shuts himself in the little room and eats to his heart's content. If another family member goes over to eat at the same time and jiggles the closed door, the one inside will stick his left pinky toe outside and jiggle it back. This gesture is approximately comparable to our traditional "Occupied!"

Speaking of which, this little-room business has been the cause of great immorality among the children. It's not uncommon for parents to catch boys and girls of up to seven years of age eating together!

These are in broad strokes the ways of the Pacaás Novos. I've left out lots of things: that they are extremely strict about the notion of virginity (as it relates to the ear); that they accept polygamy and that their great marubixaba[62] had seventy speech-wives, etc. Maybe I'll tell that story another day. I do know that they live happily. They are very active and decently filthy, as we understand filthiness, very docile and affectionate, tho their insistence on talking with kicks has left my leg quite blue.

Inaspiteof my terrible curiosity I left there quickly, because of the smell of the, shall we say, hexpectorations, piled up on the ground, inside the homes, everywhere. I'm worried I didn't make myself clear since I wrote that when I arrived the children were naked, and indeed they were, but not because those things were showing. They were naked because the younguns are innocent things, they say, there's no harm in them showing their chins, even their ears, and that divinely sinful thing that we call the mouth.

Let me relate just one more thing, which by the way the interpreter repeated to me only far away from the rest. It should be clear by now that a woman showing a man her lip is the height of shamelessness. Well, not too long ago there was a great sensation among the depraved members of the tribe, a Pacaá dancer who, in a sort of cabaret erected by herself a league and a half from the village, had advertised nude performances, appearing entirely clothed but with her mouth visible, singing Neapolitan ditties she'd learned from a Peruvian river peddler who had taken her ear. The racket was so terrific that the pajé[63] was forced to deliver a fiery leg-shaking sermon against these excesses. The women of the tribe, hopping mad, got together in a fury and went and ate the dancer.

JUNE 9

Life on board. Early in the morning we stopped at Manacapuru, which I didn't see since I was dreaming. Today's snack was sapotilha, biriba, a Brazilian apricot, which is another thing entirely, and cupuaçu juice—now what language is this! Afternoon: wooding station. As always, I got off, and the little

farm was called Felicidade. The resident had a way with words,
I should say, and he'd also put up this sign: "ATTENTION,
GOOD SIRS! I got orders from the baws to not SELL nothin
on credit. Followin orders is real nice." We tried unripe cacao
fruit—not worth it. Furious mosquito invasion. At night, a
dance on board: clarinet, two guitars, a cavaquinho, and a
ganzá. All of the above in third class.

*The farm was called
Felicidade.*

JUNE 10

Life on board. Too many children, I even dreamed about the
little lambs having their throats cut. In the morning we stopped
at Codajás, where I took a stroll with Schaeffer, looking for a
bird taxidermist who's famous around these parts. He was Italian and a painter, poor thing. He had an admirably well-stuffed
harpy eagle. On board, Scales, Trumpet, and I tried out the
language of flowers, using a book acquired in Manaus. Logs
rolling by under the steamer's flat bottom. Another dead alligator, festooned with vultures. And always those little islands of
grass, periantãs, they're called, drifting downstream. They say
the grass just grows that way, feeding off whatever it finds in
the water—I can't swear to it. Up on the roof of the boat, we
sang in the moonlight, Trumpet on the guitar, after we'd fled

from the dance. The moon is immense and so is our breast. Two hybrid orchids, French lavender and scarlet carnation.[64]

THE RUBBER PROBLEM

You can struggle against ignorance and defeat it. You can struggle against culture and at the very least be understood by it, explained by it. With the prejudice of the semi-cultured there can be no hope of victory or comprehension. Ignorance is a rock: it breaks. Culture is a void: it takes things in. But semi-culture? It's a pest with the consistency of rubber: it gives way, then bounces back.

JUNE 11

In the small hours we were swallowed up by such a formidable fog that the steamer stopped. It only got going again after sunup and headed over toward the mouth of the Mamiá, where there was a nice-looking farm, picturesque as could be—cue a great flurry of getting ready. The owner of the farm was nowhere to be seen, he had leprosy. The woman, another leper, was on board with us, we've found out only just now. Their children too. This gave the landscape an absolutely ghastly air, and of course nobody even thought of getting off. There's no other place we won't stop, tho. And then nothing for it but to splash ourselves down with cachaça to knock out the chiggeration. Round about noon we got off at the pretty little village of Coari, feeling ready to cut loose. Everything was pretty, everyone was healthy, the bridge gracious. We bought nuts and ate nuts galore. Hot. We set off, towing a big canoe and the fruit seller, a black man, who flags down the Amazon River Company ships by firing off a little cannon. Today we talked at length with the genius on board. At first we thought he was crazy, but no, everyone swears he's a genius. He also seems to be a con artist, but I'll skip that experience. It's astounding that a ship as big as a ship should stop in a tiny place called São Luís just to deliver a letter. I'm not punning: that's just the size it is, really.

DRIFTING ON THE RIVER, ONE P.M.

I like the river's abundant solitude. Nothing pleases me more than to be by myself and look at the river in the fullness of day, deserted. It's extraordinary how everything bubbles up with beings, with gods, with indescribable beings behind it all, especially if the yonder in front of me is a bend in the river. Not just here along the Amazon, but especially on smaller rivers, like the Tietê, the Moji. It catches you short. The river changes course at the end of a long straight stretch, an indiscernible mass of greens bars the horizon, and everything fills up with the living mysteries that hide themselves away in there. At each instant I feel that the revelation is bound to come—grandiose, terrible, just around the river bend. And then somehow I've got company, my own company, more dangerous than it is good, aching with fears I know are unfounded but are still real, vague, and all the more consummate and indisputable for it, legitimate fears of the phenomenal danger of living (of existing). But all it takes is someone coming over, a voice drifting up from first class, and the spell evaporates.

In São Paulo too, in the sought-out solitudes I cherish so much, at night down the sleeping streets, everything around me always fills up—with people, with beings. But on those occasions, urban reality imposes more utilitarian presences: they're always either characters I make up in order to have peaceful happy stories with, or they're my partners in life, my friends. But these friends are always better than my flesh-and-blood friends, the same in name and body but improved by yours truly. Even in my study, I find it pleasant when I'm writing . . . It's not just the question, or answer, that we artists pose to ourselves as we create something—"What will Carlos Drummond think of this?" "Manuel Bandeira will like this poem"—no. That's more of a yearning for an applaudatory presence, and you feel it only after a work of art is finished. What I feel, or what I do while I'm writing, or even reading, is to have the room inhabited by usually one, and on rare occasions two friends, who are there, I swear they are, reading over my shoulder as I write, giving me advice, guiding me, contradicting me out of a spirit of friendship and dedication to firm up my arguments. There's nothing better . . . I don't enjoy paradoxes, which are the province of people who have all sorts of complexes and wield them to avenge themselves on the painful contradiction that stands between the external reality of life and said complexes: but it's true that I never feel quite so abandoned, savoring the barren taste of loneliness, as when I am in a room full of people, even if they are all my friends. There's no getting around it: I like my friends far better when they're far away from me.

JUNE 12

A breezy day, sublime. The most ridiculous aspect of this human race of ours is that each individual has his own personal knack. One can crow like a rooster, another can wiggle his ears, and so on. On board, everyone shows theirs off! We stopped in a little place called Caiambé, with the kapok trees growing up out of the water, at a beautiful farm called Centenário, a little blue house, and then at São Isidoro Farm, delivering another letter. During the day, Teffé—why on earth did I put two fs!—where Scales and I bet on who could become the most sartorially ridiculous. I won by a mile, of course, I'm a man, and we caused the biggest fuss. Life on board. River dolphins fun-fun-funning around in the afternoon, eating fish. The dolphins eat fish in the afternoons like that, just for fun. Night had already fallen when we came to a wooding station. The equatorial sky, ruled over by Ursa Major, the great Saci . . .[65] We were in a frenzy, hankering for crimes, even. Back off the lake was a little spot, Caiçara, where a party was going on. We went over and caught a "Ciranda" dance that I saw almost the whole way through, wrote down two songs on a cigarette packet, and took notes as best I could, since I'd forgotten my notebook. It was nearly into the wee hours when the steamer started mooing off in the distance, letting us know that it was waiting for us. I must note that, when necessary, the heads of the company kindly set to Dona Olívia's desires the schedules for the steamers we're traveling on. We danced with the caboclos and made our way back at our leisure, through the night of the Great Bear. Sublime day.

THE CIRANDA
(NOTES AS THEY WERE TAKEN)[66]

All in the wedding scene, priest imitated Arab-talk, thinking he was imitating Latin. Gives a communion wafer—"That girl bit me! She thought it was a hunk of manatee!"—After wedding, the Limpkin comes in, all gather round. "Here comes the ciranda—the Limpkin's death is nigh!" (repeat). The bird comes into the circle and the hunter, from outside it, tries to kill it. He shoots. Limpkin wounded. Priest protests: "Don't hit the Limpkin in the head!" etc. (The ciranda made it possible to escape death.) Limpkin dead, priest commends the deceased. Puts stole on Limpkin's head, bird resuscitates. All danced with clapping. Accompanied by guitar and cavaquinho. Syncopated rhythms. Red blouses hemmed with blue, turbans with flowers and feathers. Faces painted red with urucum. Then departure from the home of Mr. Teófilo Nojes (can't read my handwriting) with the "Ciranda, cirandinha" circle dance song, traditional.

JUNE 13

Morning stop at a farm, Boca do Aiucá, with music! What's this now? It was a dance. They'd been dancing since afternoon the day before, and things might go on for "a few days yet." Lots of the men from the dance came to load firewood onto the steamer (there was a station), and most of the women waited.

Then they kept on dancing, women with women. They trade off instinctively. Someone gets hungry and goes off to eat, and someone gets tired and goes off to sleep. The orchestra was playing a plain, wailing chorinho, with violin, cavaquinho, and all sorts of invented percussion, like a stick beating on a bottle. I tried cocona preserves—a nice sharp acidic taste, the flesh delicate and very soft. But you can feel the jungle, biting hard into your tongue. It isn't eaten raw. The fruit is an old red color, shaped like a June plum. It was raining. On the farm we saw maguari storks, curassows, yellow-rumped caciques, herons. There was a corral of turtles, too. Have a cold, a bit feverish.

Siri-pintanha: a mother with no father for her child.

Embiara: food. "Going to get me some embiara out in the forest." A fellow who's bossed around (by his master, his employer, an enemy who's stronger) calls the other one his "jaguar." The dominator calls the dominated one embiara: "This here is my embiara." Rio Branco region.

JUNE 14

Woke up well. Morning stop in Fonte Boa, note the placement of the adjective. Outing with mayor and family. Dona Olívia wielding her movie camera. To please them, she asked the mayor, wife, and their ten children to "make their way over" for her to cinematograph them. Make their way they did, in one of the most majestically distressing sights I've ever seen. The woman was so overcome that she couldn't even move her legs and eventually just fell over. Swear to God.

This old life on board. Remarkable greenery weeping in vines down to the river water. Astounding sunset. Squirrel monkeys. At the mouth of the Jutaí we saw a simply beautiful Indian woman, a perfect Asian type. We were sitting there, waiting for word to come back from the rubber plantation down the Jutaí. Whenever the steamer comes by a place it keeps up relations with, takes goods and correspondence from, etc., it whistles from a distance as it comes. The interested party isn't the only one within earshot, and so out pop boats with folks who've come, my God! to see people from civilizations, Manaus, Belém, the world. And they're joined by Indians, those tame Indians who're completely Brazilian by now and go around speaking our tongue, perhaps with no memory of their tribes. Well, that's what happened. They came over in a dugout, she and her man, and stayed at a distance, some thirty meters away, taking a look, not asking for anything, not saying anything, not coming over, just taking a look. The fellow, it was clear, was more experienced—he talked, gesticulated, showed things. She barely moved, barely even looked at the ship. Me with my binoculars on her. Not just me! Schaeffer, the man from Rio Grande do Sul, the postman from Manaus, the eye-talian Humpity-Hump, which isn't a naughty name, just the girls poking fun, because in Belém he didn't want to go swimming with us and eventually let on that it was because he had a deformed foot, with one toe "humped up" over the other one. Well, I didn't catch the marvelous Indian woman looking at the ship once, eyes always cast down. She was wearing a skirt, a woman's skirt, gathered at her bare waist, and a sort of scarlet shirt (the skirt was a dark color) falling in pleats down to her midriff. Only as they left did we realize that the shirt was only in front, covering her breasts. Behind there was only a little ruffle over her shoulders, with her back showing.

It's entertaining at first, but ultimately hellish, how muddled the information we get about local things is—hard to believe. Every last person casts himself as a terrific connoisseur of this pompous Amazonia, which for them is the source of a fantastic, improbable vanity, "the land of the future" . . . But when you get down and ask about a thing, one will tell you it's a Brazil-nut tree and another will argue it's duck in tucupi sauce. The only people who know anything at all are the ignorant folks in third class. Save with the modernists in Rio, I've rarely seen a bunch with such a thoroughly cockeyed education—most of them speaking English.

JUNE 15

A full day. A bit Swissified in the past few days, after a number of conversations with Schaeffer; I'm getting used to coming up on the roof of the steamer to watch the birth of day, to let myself be utterly sublimed by it. But today's sublime dawn brought us quite a dramatic scene. There's an old man on board, in third class, who had a cerebral congestion that left him out of his wits. But he's a gentle soul, doesn't bother anyone, doesn't talk. Just one time he came over and handed Dona Olívia a filthy kerchief full of Brazil nuts. And then he walked away without asking for a thing! Apparently, this morning (meaning this dawn), apparently he was agitated, pacing up and down endlessly. All of a sudden, spotting a man in a canoe on the other bank, he shouted, "Goodbye, Jó," getting no answer. Another man in another canoe, about two hundred meters on, and the maniac: "Goodbye, Jó! Goodbye, Jó!"—no answer. The steamer scraping by the riverbank, a fairly populated part, since we'd soon stop at Tonantins. And whenever anyone appeared, he'd start hollering out into the morning: "Goodbye, Jó!" But nobody answered. Nobody took pity, nobody contrived up the pity to answer. I asked him who Jó was. (We'd already passed the Bugarim fork.)

"My son," he answered. "He lives here. Used to live here . . ."

Meanwhile, a ruined shack drew close, falling to pieces, nobody in it. A few vestiges of a garden out front. The man pulled the kerchief out of his pocket and, gesticulating widely, waved goodbye. The shack disappearing into the distance, him in silence, making those broad gestures, waving goodbye, waving goodbye. I asked where he was headed.

"To Remate de Males,[67] yessir. A ways farther down . . . I had congestion, y'know? I got better, but all my eyes want is to shut! I've got three kids . . ."

"Are they there?"

"They're around . . ."

"But don't you have family in Remate de Males?"

"A ways farther down . . . round there . . . But don't you

know some medicine so my eyes don't want to shut no more? Please, sir!"

I retreated, I couldn't take it anymore.

It was ring-kissing time. It's plain to see: plenty of people feel proud and understandably pleased to chum around with our important traveling companion. A funny sight. Round about nine o'clock, the Coffee Queen would make her appearance, always all gussied up, that smile of hers on the tip of her lips, bestowed on one and all. An hour beforehand, you'd see a horde of passengers circling her cabin in search of a good-morning.

Now and then you'd see sheets of thick mud streaking the surface of the river. It was slime from the riverside lagoons, sucked out as the waters begin to fall.

We went by the famous beach of Bom Jardim, which still produces between three and five thousand turtles a year. Mujanguê: river-turtle eggs beaten with flour and salt. The same treat made with sugar instead of salt is called arabu. "Sweet little Caraboo . . ."[68]

Nothing more apropos—we're coming up to Tonantins, a wooding station with a Franciscan mission, but which provided us with a concert of bel canto. Two lovely Italian friars, fat, strong, and chortling. We were visiting the installations—a school with forty enrolled students, a malaria prophylactic station (shut down since the Government stopped sending medicine), the little church, and a field out back with a little garden and guava trees—when Brother Diogo came up, making a hullabaloo and inviting us into the priests' quarters. We went in. Clean, hygienic, coffee. In the living room, a piano. Without even asking who we were, Brother Diogo went ahead and invited us to make some music. I was tempted to examine some manuscripts of Tantum Ergo and Kyrie, which were nevertheless clearly not religious. I played them, and they were really no good. Trumpet, flipping through other music piled up on the piano lid, found I Lombardi and "Musetta's Waltz." Just for fun, I started singing the waltz. Dolur turned up maxixes by Eduardo Souto that I went for with no prompting and played in chorus with Trumpet and Scales. We found Toselli—nothing more opportune—performed with great feeling in a duet, Trumpet and me. Brother Diogo, who'd gone off to fetch something or other, came back in and was ecstatic. He jumped for joy and forced us to do an encore. Scales, guffawing, turned up the Fashist hymn, which was performed mockingly by all, Brother Diogo pitching in, in as out-of-tune a chorus as we could muster from our throats. After the "Giovinezza," we asked Brother Diogo to sing. He gave in, tremendously flattered, and sang a chorus from *Nabucco*, solo, as I accompanied him on the piano. An admirable voice, for that matter. Coffee. Brother Antonino came in. Brother Diogo made a hullabaloo (everything was a hullabaloo with these two Italians) letting us know that the other priest could sing too. Brother Antonino made a hullabaloo claiming that he had "the voice of a burro," but for our sake, he'd sing "Santa Lucia." I accompanied him. A booming voice, for open-air theater. And then Trumpet again, our delightful prima donna, and "Chuá-chuá" and "Casinha da colina," the two friars making an unbearable hullabaloo. They were all bliss. At this point, Captain Garcia, a sort of factotum they gave us in Belém—quite a delightful one at that—told the friars that we were from São Paulo. Silence struck the two hullabalooers. They looked at us respectfully, and we felt in the yearning eyes of those two exiles a nostalgia, a longing for the homeland of all the eye-talians in the world. But Brother Diogo soon recovered:

"You all are Paulistas . . . you're not Brazilians! To be Brazilian, you've got to come by Amazonas, this is the place! You [he pointed at me] pronounce things just like an Italian." I told him that, indeed, I was the son and grandson of Italians.

"Fashista?"

"Antifashista!" I replied.

At this the friar made a hullabaloo and went to get the mail for the mission that had come on our steamer. He opened up the packet and waved at us, making a hullabaloo, with a copy of *Squilla*, an antifashist paper from São Paulo, which they subscribed to. And the other, the only daily in the world they subscribed to, *O Estado de S. Paulo*—I swear I felt a thrill, half state pride, half astonishment at the importance of the

Estado. We said goodbye, and the two friars, with the most indecent innocence, pulled us into bear hugs, intimate as could be. On board, dinner was on the table. The Tapuios had already hauled twenty thousand logs onto the ship, and the commander was taking advantage of their cheery disposition to see if they could make it to forty thousand. As we were eating dinner, Brother Antonino came up making a hullabaloo. I asked. He didn't think that the Amazonian caboclos were innately religious, no. Mostly indifferent and had to be treated very carefully lest they cut and run from mass. Mainly content with owning a picture of Santo Antônio, and that's that. Or of Nossa Senhora. But they don't pray or trouble themselves much with God. But they're happier than you civilized folk. No ambition whatsoever. A little flour, a lot of cachaça, and they're happy. They have a mess of kids. And that's all they need. Happier than you civilized folk, to be sure. But some of them have horrible festivities. When it's just dancing, that's all right enough. They just got done with Santo Antônio, which is thirteen nights of dancing, no thought of doing away with that! But "certain sorts" of caboclos have a celebration, for example, called Moça Nova (I looked at the girls, snickering) that you wouldn't believe! . . . Silence fell for a long while. The ship was about to set off, which was as good an excuse as any to keep him from wallowing in melancholy thoughts of the Festa da Moça Nova. And Brother Antonino bid us farewell from the gangway and left. In a hullabaloo.

JUNE 16

Sublime small hours up on the top of the steamer. Early in the morning, we stopped to cut swamp grass for the cattle. A pair of macaws flies across the river. Flutters of yellow butterflies along the river's skin. Suddenly a blue one, one of the big ones. Dragonflies galore. And the fish jumpity-jumping in the backwaters. And all the tinamous, don't people hunt those birds around here? They call out to me with a chirp, I answer, and so I spend hours flirting with no shotgun as the greenery brushes

by and more roving lands. Maturá, a lovely little village where
you can go mountain climbing. Fantastically hot day. In the afternoon we stopped at São Paulo de Olivença, with its chatty
mayor, his school-age daughter, and Brother Fidélis. We were
visiting the school, the Colégio Nossa Senhora da Assunção,
and the teacher, a respectable old lady showing every bit of her
age, filled in as our Baedeker.[69] Since we exchanged a few English words, she got to speaking English—better than me, that's
a cinch, but with greater ease and much more confidence than
the girls. Just now she was showing us the litters and all the
rest, the flowers, veils, and queen's wreaths from a procession
that morning, and when we were taken aback by her perfect
English, she told us with a bit of melancholy that she had been
a virgin in London and Paris—truly heroic. Back in the hands
of Brother Fidélis, I saw the *Estado de S. Paulo* and the *Men-
sageiro do Coração de Jesus*, from Itu, São Paulo. In Tefé the
Portuguese grocer swore I was Portuguese born and bred, in
Tonantins I passed for Italian, and now, here in São Paulo de
Olivença, Brother Fidélis asks me hesitantly if I'm English or
German! Sublime night with a full moon. The seagulls that
come down on the floating logs are woken up by the steamer's
panting and make an unbelievable racket. At two in the morning, we stop in Santa Rita to buy tucum-fiber hammocks. Terrifically fun day.

JUNE 17

At the crack of dawn we stopped at the Assacaio wooding station, an extraordinarily interesting place. Schaeffer and I ventured into the forest and supplied ourselves with curious
objects, including a beautiful parrot's-beak flower.[70] I cut
down, and am carrying with me, a piece of the so-called mata-
matá liana—the tortoise's ladder, they explain, the same one
the moon used to climb up to the sky. Man improving on the
pirarucu caught this evening. Pirarucu have their hearts in
their throats. Roses pouring out perfume, never seen anything
like it. Legitimate Indians playing at blacks, painted with

genipap. They don't paint their finger joints, which makes them look like pale scars, it's horrible. I photoed it. Shortly after noon we landed at Assacaio, where we saw some beautiful Indians, especially one forlorn girl, well into womanhood, a splendidly delicate figure. At night I was overcome with a wretched fit of irritation, and no wonder. The fellow from Rio Grande do Sul who's joined our Amazonian voyage and lives in São Paulo has delusions of grandeur: "Take me, for instance. When I buy boots at the best shop, it'll set me back two hundred mil-réis. This suit I got at Lattuchella's—nine hundred." The poor folk are thunderstruck, I can't tell if they're buying it. Then the megalomaniac turned to me and asked if that wasn't the plain truth. And I . . . I said it was. I don't really know why, but my leg was itching so bad from the chiggers and I was so out of sorts, I said that he was right and ran with it— any little shack in São Paulo would cost you six hundred to rent, a square meter downtown went for a hundred thousand and nobody was selling, I made seven thousand a month and could barely afford a thing, and everyone looked on the verge of laughing. Then I turned to the man and hit him right on the jaw with it: "Isn't that right?"

To repay the debt he had to say that it was, and I had my revenge. I felt so relieved that the itching stopped (that was all, tho), and I went off to drink a cold glass of guaraná to see if it'd calm my nerves. In these parts, I've learned to scratch myself in three different ways: objectively, subjectively, and physio-psychically, which is the best of all. Around midnight, the girl who's in love with everyone came down. A hellish night. On top of everything, the mosquitoes harassed me so thoroughly I thought I'd go crazy.

"What's that out there? An alligator, you think?"

"Cain't say, cain't rightly see . . . But sho' looks like it."

Coming back from the outing at Assacaio. The monster shows itself.

JUNE 18

Arrived at Esperança, the Brazilian customs post. Just across from the Peruvian shore. Went down the Javari, headed for Remate de Males. The taxizeiro trees have polychromatic flowers that start out scarlet and descend by degrees into orange pink, pale rose, whitish yellow, light greenish, and finally an out-and-out lettuce green. Put like that it sounds pretty, but the truth is it's not attractive. This treeling is home to the twig ant. Remate de Males at one-thirty. The chapel with a metal-clad church tower. Remate-de-Malevolently hot. The biggest building around is the Masonic temple, and everyone wound up becoming Masons because of it. At one store:

"Got any alcohol?"

"Nossir."

"Isn't there a straw hat, an oar, anything made here that could be a souvenir?"

"Nossir, nobody makes nothin' out in this accurst land."

Eventually we came across a couple with malaria, leaning out their window, and their family at the door, malarial as all get-out too.

"How many children do you have?"

"Twelve, señor . . . hard to keep 'em fed in this accurst land."

A bit farther on: "Kid, do you know who sells bananas around here?"

"Ain't got none!"

"What do you mean, none! There's only none if nobody plants them!"

"Ah . . . it's an accurst land."

The heat was accurst, all right. We went back on board. From the very start of the outing, we'd been deprived of Dona Olívia's company. After not even ten steps on land, she'd beaten a retreat to her cabin so as not to see those people, every last one of them eaten away at by malaria. As we arrived back on board, a motorboat made its way over from the Peruvian bank. A dark-skinned Peruvian hopped out, strongly built, blood bright behind his dark skin. He talked, talked, and took over the ship.

And I felt an aching for malaria, for a malaria that would obliterate every curiosity in my body and spirit. Here's what happened. Soon as we came back on board, Trumpet came over in a tizzy to say that a marvelously handsome fellow was at the bar. That's always how it is: whenever the steamer stops at a port, all the best-quality folks in town come on board. Then they stay awhile. We went to see the young man in question, and he did have an extraordinarily beautiful face, looking a bit like Richard Barthelmess. But completely hollowed out by malaria, and his skin, smooth as could be, was an earthy brown with no pleasure in it. The girls got all frisky, and since everyone was always watching and fancying them, they started doing their utmost to make the young man at least turn his head and catch a glimpse of them. Well, he didn't look over. No matter the racket we made, nothing was interesting enough to merit even a little look-see. He paid for his drink and left without looking. The girls went after him. He, leaning up against the railing, looked out ahead. The girls got to walking up and down the deck, chatting away loudly, in a fantastically saucy display of butting in. What did the young man do? Didn't look over, got off and walked away without looking back one solitary time. That was when I yearned for a malaria like that, so nothing would ever interest me, in this world in which everything interests me far more than it should . . .

We stopped again, back at Esperança to take on firewood. Night had fallen. We heard about a little dance nearby, a wedding party, and we headed over there—the customs officer from Manaus, the two girls, and me. We were going along in an absurdly small canoe that barely sat the four of us, the lip of the boat flush with the water. And a rainstorm broke, a terrific one. We were forced to beach the boat as best we could and dash along the path to the house, which we could make out about fifty meters up. We got there soaked to the bone and the party stopped on our account—oh, servile hospitality . . . The pretty bride and her mother went to take care of the girls, gave them clothes as they heated up an iron to steam their jodhpurs and shirts. The groom restless, not knowing what to do with me. The party adjourned. Then they offered us drinks—wine fortified with quinine, and aluá, with its agreeably sour tang, overly perfumed with cinnamon. We toasted to the bride and groom and the dance started up again to the sound of a flute, the enemy of a stout guitar that puffed and panted trying to keep up as the flute scampered here and there. The groom got up, took the bride by the hand, brought her over, and offered her up to dance with me—isn't that wonderful! And he went off to dance with Trumpet. Then he danced with Scales. And we stayed, dancing to the sound of the two instruments and a soldier who sang with his eyes cast down out of sheer embarrassment—I don't think he looked at us a single time. And to think he was a soldier! The steamer bellowed down below, calling us. The moon was out. Someone had gone to fetch our little boat, which was down at the port. And we drifted downriver in the moonlight, singing "Luar do sertão"

(Country Moon), puffed up with romantic feeling, a good sort of ache in our hearts.

It was almost three in the morning and the Coffee Queen had turned in long ago. We woke up the barman, aiming to have a snifter of something strong to ward off a cold. I had my nip and went off to my cabin to change out of my soaked clothes, leaving the girls with the customs officer. I wasn't gone fifteen minutes, but as soon as I got back to the bar, I saw the damage. The fellow had made some sort of bet with the girls, and they, with their overfree upbringing, had drunk far too much, glass after glass of cachaça. I dispatched everyone off to bed, and before too long a suspicious racket started up in the girls' cabin, which shared a wall with mine on one side and Dona Olívia's maid's on the other. The racket grew steadily louder. Trumpet was wailing and Scales was calling my name, between shrieks of laughter. I was bothered to no end—if the Queen was to wake up and investigate, she'd find the two of them completely drunk. And I'd been swallowing all sorts of things since the start of the trip, to spare Dona Olívia any unpleasantness . . .

"Oh, what is it, Scales! Please, keep it down!"

Now I heard Trumpet, even clearer now, bawling out and calling me. I got dressed in a hurry and went out on deck. What was I to see! Their cabin door wide open, Scales lying on the floor, Trumpet on the bed and Scales yanking at her legs. Trumpet hadn't been able to get one of her boots off, not even with Scales's help, and what now? A light went on in Dona Olívia's cabin, and I was stricken with fear. The light went out. But if someone saw me go in or out of the girls' cabin—they had such a bad reputation as it was, all because of their modern liberties! And Trumpet's wails seemed only to be getting louder. And Scales's failed attempts were making her roll across the cabin floor, stifling more and more laughter. The light goes on again—it's Dona Olívia. I warn them with a gesture. The light goes off, ah, I couldn't take it anymore! Dying as you dither? Rather a death by daring, I muttered along with Bocage,[71] damned it all inwardly, went in, and yanked off Trumpet's boot. Felt like giving them a slap.

JUNE 19

Five in the morning, Tabatinga, last Brazil, which I saw in dreams. At six, first Peru, Leticia,[72] only glimpsed. At ten we landed at Victoria, the sugar mill owned by the Peruvian Dr. Vigil, lovely installations, progressive, spick-and-span, an air of happiness. I tried quince—a boring little fruit, tasted silly. Peruvians are all born in Italy: they gesticulate and make a hullabaloo. This Dr. Vigil proved himself a stupendous fellow in a second flat. Strong, optimistic, good-hearted, affectionate, courteous, patriotic, knowledgeable—whatever he doesn't know, he'll make up. In the course of two years, he set up this extraordinary sugar mill. We visited all of the two hundred seven million skeeters that Dr. Vigil breeds with the help of two hundred forty Indians that he managed to domesticate and make work efficiently. We Peruvians, it's enough to make you proud—you're barely out of poor bedraggled Brazil, with no intrepid initiative to call its own, rotting out in this big old world of water, you barely stick your fork into Peru, and there you have a gorgeous initiative, the most modern machinery imported from Englands and United Stateses and so on, machines all over, running on Peruvian blood and Zuloaga paintings. We set off flush with enthusiasm after a visit to the lumber mill, the sugar mill, and a tour of the canefields in wagons drawn by trotting Quechuas—Juan and Manuelito, I felt like a toreador. Dr. Vigil, incidentally, is coming along with us to Iquitos, and has already taken the place of Professor Hagmann's phonograph next to the Coffee Queen. Who smiles patiently all the while.

JUNE 20

Stopped in the wee hours at a wooding station, Chimbote. On board, a bunch of malarial youngsters. Around lunchtime we went by San Pablo, a leper colony with its little bathhouses down by the riverside . . .[73] Life on board. First naked adult Indian spotted. Dr. Vigil's charm is becoming unsustainable.

At one point he talked about alligators twelve meters long! It's remarkable to hear him tell the story of the war the Peruvians had with the Chileans.[74] From day one, the Peruvians gave the Chileans a beating, you had to see it, they didn't lose one skirmish, one ambush, it was just one thrashing after another. In the end they lost the war. And you wouldn't believe the hatred—speak of a Chilean and a Peruvian's eyes shoot daggers. Howlers on the branches.

JUNE 21

Life on board. We're bracing ourselves for arrival at Iquitos, *la gran capital de la provincia de Loreto*, official visit, official welcome . . . Now and then a long firm whistle pierces the green of the forest, and what is it! Indians. Civilized Indians sending word on ahead that there's a steamer coming by. Beaches that come to float in the ebb, warming themselves in the sun. And now shall I say what happened? I won't. I just know that I had a tremendous blowup with the captain of the steamer, the doctor, all these Brazilians treading on other folks' soil. But I gave them a hell of an earful. Quiet folks like me are like that, when we fly off the handle we really go flying, so I cursed them all and left, slamming the door of the captain's cabin. And I went to have it out with the son of a gun, none other than the captain, *el gran capitán Carrillo, jefe del puerto de Iquitos*, I walked up to him, cold and bloodless, and said, I don't know where the voice came from, I said: "Sir, step aside or I'll put six bullets in your craw!"

Later I laughed at that—not only did I not have a revolver, I'm also not sure the captain had any idea what a craw was. And I stayed there, leaning up against the railing—this was after dinner—in front of our cabins, which were the first on the left, near the bow. Time for a postprandial stroll, everyone walking along the ship's deck. The gran capitán went walking around with his eleven-year-old son too, sulking, looking like he was fixing to be furious. And me calm, up against the railing, back to the river, watching folks on their constitutional.

After a while some sat down, others went into the saloon, others to the bar. The captain strolling. Me there, standing firm. Did I think it? Man alive! There was a cold calm in me, the fatalism of those who have no courage whatsoever but are incapable of backing down if the time really does come. Whenever the captain came by, I'd follow him with my eyes from the moment he appeared in the distance to the moment he rounded the corner. But he didn't look at me one bit—if he did, I'd ask, "What are you looking at?" dead-on. The girls found out, apparently the retired captain traveling with Dona Olívia told them, they're ashen and trying to hide it, they've come to ask me not to do anything, anything at all!

"Go away, now! Act natural so Dona Olívia doesn't notice."

Me calm, always in the same place. Some go into their cabins. Silence falls, bit by bit, on board. And me calm. Calm, hooey! In hell, pretending to be calm. The captain strolling, scowlier all the time. The boy, his son, has been in bed a while now. We spent hours that way. By morning we'll be in Iquitos. Hours on hours, I even got distracted from what I was doing, I just haven't got a warlike bone in me, I started thinking about something else. Suddenly, with a start—what, where'd he go? I paid attention. He wasn't coming round anymore. I thought: of course, he's gone to bed. A thought that I "of course" followed up with a tremendous curse word directed at Captain Carrillo, the captain of the port of Iquitos, who after all was traveling on board the steamer *São Salvador*, treading on Brazilian soil. And fatalism is a strange thing: coldly, with no desire, no anger, I went over there, I did, walked over to the other side of the ship, in front of Carrillo's cabin, making my feet ring out on the floor. And then I went to lie down, how tired I was! not a drop of courage in me, my soul aching, nerved up so as it couldn't bear to be touched. Even so it occurred to me that at least I'd been in one place, nice and leaning for all those hours of anguish, while poor Carrillo must've walked about three leagues around the deck. I didn't feel one bit like laughing, but I laughed.

JUNE 22

Iquitos in the morning. *Siembren algodón y café—Trabajen la goma elástica.*[75] Official-welcome botherations, a hundred introductions. The governor, all in white, a peruanito chiquitito, comes up, goes into the saloon, sits down, exchanges thirty-four words with Dona Olívia, springs up militarily, and leaves. Then his secretary or something lets me know that he's waiting at the mansion for us to repay the visit in precisely two hours' time! Like monarchs in London or Italy, all hail protocol! It's so hot here! People had said that the heat was worse in Iquitos than in Manaus. And skeeters, *aquí se llaman zancudos,*[76] in the middle of the day. I dry myself off and when I'm done, I'm dripping with sweat. And the heat! and the zancudos! . . . Man alive! I know I sat down on the bed, the wind out of my sails, and felt like bawling, crying out for Mama . . . At the mansion, a natty reception all in white. I had to repeat the ad lib I'd done for the first time in Belém and repeated several times since, whenever I was faced with a speech for Dona Olívia. But this time, when it came time to say that we no longer felt bound by "state borders," I changed it to "national borders," and it went over just as well. Lunch on board. We explored at our leisure. Around here, there's no customs restrictions on the industries that the Peruvians are honest enough to admit they don't have: ooh, how lovely! Swiss chocolates and all sorts of other European preserves, dirt cheap . . . *Chicha helada, un real*: sorry-tasting, like watered-down aluá.[77] And the Chinese, caramba! MODUS VIVENDI, *carpintería de António Bardales.* ZAPATERÍA, *de Juan Chiong.*[78] Iquitos is packed with viudas, widows wearing their veils down the brick-paved streets. Beautiful houses tiled in all colors. We've decided, the girls and I, to call the captain of our boat Hideous Poxie. Telegram 102 mil-réis. *Siembren algodón y café—Trabajen la goma elástica* is written on the sidewalks. Two Americans, bursting with Peruvian patriotism, write those sorts of things on the streets at night so they can do a lot of business right away and get back home sweet home. A shred of Peruvian goes by, with a massive pair of sideburns hanging off his malaria. There are almost no blacks around here, we haven't seen one yet. Suddenly here's one, or is it? A photographic negative, that's the image I'm left with: hands and face black, all the rest white, a perfect negative. We're accompanied by the Brazilian consul, a deaf, dim Mellito. Panama hat, seventy mil-réis. Dinner on land with Saavedra Pinón, quite decent. Avocado salad, eaten for the first time. At eleven P.M. we leave for Nanay.

JUNE 23

Morning found us in Santa María de Nanay, but I didn't get up right away, worried as I was with Dona Olívia's slumping social status. In Manaus she was still a queen. In Remate de Males they called her a countess. Yesterday *El Día*, in Iquitos, informed Peruvians of the arrival of "Dra." [*sic*] Olívia Penteado. They're loading mahogany onto the boat, two hundred logs of caoba, each weighing two to three tons, I'm told. *Caoba* is Spanish; here in the region the word is *aguano*, and we call it *mogno* . . . They're going to Boston, to a Victrola factory. We're in the middle of the lake, taking in the inviting view, São Paulish in its own way, with its little hills and pipe-stem palms. We go on land to visit a nearby Huitoto Indian pueblo—Dona Olívia, the two girls, a little American lady from Iquitos, and me. What passed for a port, or rather a dock, was a moored canoe about half a meter from the beach, a muddy, practically vertical slope. I jumped into the canoe, planted one foot in it and another in the mud on shore, and gave my hand to Dona Olívia. She unthinkingly jumps straight over to the sheer slope, slips, falls to her knees, and only that because I grabbed her arm. There was a moment of panic, with her struggling on her knees and using her one free hand to scrabble at the muddy soil, and as it gave way it seemed clear she'd soon slip between the canoe and the beach and vanish into the water. At last she got her footing. Well, we disguised our disappointment as best we could with the usual "not hurt, eh?," "What on earth happened there?," putting the blame squarely on the beach and suggesting that she change shoes at the very least.

And off we went, with the guide whose teeth were black from chewing coca. The Indians' path through the forest. Whenever the guide spots a fellow from his hut, he lets out peculiar shouts, sort of like cowboy whoops. The village has become a pueblo of Indians dressing like us—that is, in trousers and jackets, or trousers and shirtsleeves—and speaking a few scraps of Spanish. Little bamboo huts roofed with admirably woven palm leaves. Two rooms mainly, one open-air and one enclosed. The big hut in the middle was the only one that looked more like a house, a single enormous room with a high roof, all made of palm-tree leaves, walls and all, with a little opening up top for the smoke to get some fresh air. Inside there were wooden structures on either side, each with a family living on it, a genuine second floor. The center of the floor is smoothed out for working, a trough to one side with manioc fermenting for a drink and on a ways an Indian girl who'd already had her hair pulled out, the short hair standing up on her head painted with genipap, making flour. Two others were plucking a parrot, tough meat, for a meal. A splendid pot, I tried my damnedest to buy it but only managed to buy another, far less interesting one. The tuxaua[79] was royally in the nude, ruminating in a hammock, when we came in. He pulled on a pair of trousers and came to greet us. Generally handsome folks. One Indian woman was beautiful, even, and we wanted to take a photograph. Nice try! "Si quieren, tienen que pagar!"[80]—giggling heartily. The Peruvian government allows the Huitotos to have this place, on the condition that they work twenty days a year . . . for themselves, planting crops. They chew coca and exist. I tried everything, I kept at them, I offered them plenty of money for a little bit of coca, but there was no way around it. And we went back on board, nobody falling down no more. Night on board with amusing Americans and Englishmen. The Peruvians, descended from the Spanish, speak with patriotic pride of the Incas, Incan civilization, Incan music. Then again, there are Brazilians looking to start a Marajoara fad.[81]

NANAY, JUNE 24

Woke in the wee hours with the racket of logs being loaded
onto the boat. It wasn't five o'clock yet, and I went out on the
deck in my pajamas to take a look-see at life. The first thing I
spotted was the sarcastic Indian from yesterday in a little dugout canoe, circling the boat. He had his eye on the deck, and as
soon as he saw me, he showed his sharp teeth in a smirk. I still
hoped I might try some coca and I motioned for him to pull his
canoe alongside our boat. That was just what he was waiting
for. I went down to the third deck, and in two oar strokes he
was by my side. I got into the canoe and told him to row into
the middle of the river. I was bent on duping the Huitoto and
getting my hands on the drug. He rowed, always smirking in a
sly way, and when the racket had become a murmur gliding
over to our waters, he commenced, in his tongue: "They told
me you make songs, and you were writing on paper."

"Yes, I do. That's why I asked you for coca. I want to write
a coca song, but how'm I supposed to without trying it?"

He chuckled sheepishly, thinking it over, then repeated
firmly: "Can't give you coca, don't got none."

"Come off it! I already told you, I'll give you ten *soles* if you
give me a bit. If you won't give it, I'll buy it in town!"

"In Iquitos?"

"In Iquitos."

He chuckled again, serene. "Chinamen don't sell coca yet."

"I'll find a way, don't you worry. I only asked you because
it'd be easier."

"So you will write many songs."

"Yes, I will."

"Yesterday you told that fellow with hardly any mouth left
that it was a shame you had to see us, you wished you could see
some Incas."

I was angry about not being able to get coca, so: "Yes, I did.
The Incas are a great people. You are a degraded race."

He dipped his eyes into mine, very serious. "What is *degraded*?"

"That's what you are. The Incas had great palaces. They had

gold rings, cities, emperors dressed in feathers, painting colorful animals and gods. They worked, they could weave, they
made beautiful pots, much prettier than yours. They had
laws—"

"What's *laws*?"

"They're orders that the chiefs give and we obey, and we
have to obey or we're punished. We have to follow the orders
because they're good for everyone."

"You sure?"

"Sure of what?"

"Sure they're good for everyone?" His eyes were unbearably
mischievous.

"Yes, they are. If you have a home and a wife, is it right for
another man to come and take it all away? So the emperor orders that if someone steals another fellow's house and wife, he
has to be killed: that's what a law is."

"You're going to put all that in the song, then?"

"You bet."

"We have laws too."

"But they're degraded laws, they don't do anything. What
makes you think you can sleep the day away like you do? Why
don't you make cloth, pretty vases . . . a real stone house, not
one of those dirty huts, all horribly dark inside?"

The Huitoto bristled plenty. He set off rowing in even
strokes, eyes cast down to hide the gleaming sarcasm that lived
in them. And he began to speak in a rhythm as steady as the
strokes of his oar, after he had settled his face and could look
at me seriously again. "Well, sir, you can put all that in your
song, seeing as you believe it . . . If you understood my tongue,
I'd tell you better . . . I don't know much of yours. You say
we're degraded 'cause we have no more palaces and that's
just so, but the sons of the Incas don't have no more palaces,
just huts."

"Well, that's right: they're a degraded race too!"

"No, sir! The sons of the Incas don't make any more palaces,
that's true. Had been a time they made palaces, now they don't
anymore, you see? Not 'cause the Spanish took their palaces,
the sons of the Incas are just like us, they could make more. But

the Incas made palaces, then some more, and then one day they made a palace so beautiful, so pretty that folks stopped to wonder. Then another emperor came and made another palace, and it too was so beautiful that people stopped to look. There was . . . there wasn't two palaces, there was one palace and then another palace, and people would stop and look at one palace and then stop and look at the other one . . . Each one was more beautiful than the other, the fathers of the tribes say, and it was a terrible revelation. Everyone did remark on the palaces, that they were the same thing, woven together with feathers and laws. There was all sorts of things and they were the best sorts of things, but they were even better, see. The emperor even wanted to order people to think the palace and the law he made was better, but they stopped and looked just the same, in front of one palace and the other palace; and on account of that law there was a fearful war between the emperor's soldiers and the people. When it was over, the people had won 'cause they fought without a doubt in their minds.

"Well then, they replaced the emperor with the first fellow who'd noticed that one palace couldn't be prettier than the other. Then the fellow put down a law saying nobody could build more palaces, 'cause deep down in people, when you looked, deep in the darkness, there was another palace, even more guaçu, so, so! beautiful it was impossible to build. Everyone wanted to obey the law by the fellow who knew so much, but it was impossible on account of it didn't fix anything; neither palaces nor laws made people happy. It didn't fix anything on account of if people poked around in the darkness, deep down in themselves, they'd see that beautiful palace or that law that truly did make people happy, they'd see so and they were right. But behind the beautiful palace and the perfect law, which were so big that they couldn't exist in life as it goes on, behind the palace and the law, deep down inside each person, in the darkness, there came another palace and another law that seemed even more perfect, but which people couldn't even know if they were truly more perfect on account of they were so impossibly good that people couldn't even find out which ones they were! . . . So all the people rose up, and one afternoon an angry bunch got ahold of that wise fellow and hung him in his poor hut. The sons of the Incas had known the ways of coca a long while, but a law said since forever that no-body could chew coca, only the deadly sick. The fathers of the tribes told the sons of the Incas about the palaces and they were horrified by the deaths during the war and the revolution. And just like the Huitotos, they were much wiser, since they didn't have any more wars or revolutions.

"The white man defeated us and took advantage of that. He takes advantage by giving the Huitotos land to live and making a law that Indians have to work in the fields twenty days a year. If a Huitoto had his way even twenty'd be too much. Huitotos don't even need to imagine if they're happy, on account of they're past the time of the palace and the law. Huitotos are happy, you hear, they're not degraded folk, no. Huitotos don't have laws 'cause they're happy and that's why they behave. Put coca in their mouths to eat. And they have good lives. Huitotos only know what God commands 'cause now the Huitotos have a god who orders them around. They don't bother anymore about the palace of stone or the palace that's down inside peo-ple, in the dark."

He stopped, worn out, and rowed back to the steamer. When we arrived, he said his goodbyes. "I've got coca right here in my pocket, but I won't give you none. You've got an emperor who still says not to chew coca, so what are you disobeying for! Only make you unhappier. There was no use telling you what I did, I know. It's very late, no, it's too early for you not to be unhappy . . . I said what I said for you to write a prettier song."

JUNE 24

Nanay still, with the racket of the logs being loaded on. Kind of a dull morning. Round noon, back to Iquitos. Group outing, having ice cream. Meeting with the consul, who seems to do nothing but meet us, for pity's sake! Trip on the little train through town. A poor neighborhood of pretty little houses, prettier than the Brazilian kind. Excellent dinner, genuine German beer, the best English preserves. At night, an official ball at the International Club, where the dancing still begins with the (official) quadrille. Dona Olívia dances well, with the prefect of Loreto, who I called the governor earlier. He's not, he's the prefect of the department of Loreto. The girls (I had sense enough not to dance) get everything wrong, like any modern young ladies worth their salt. Scales is overcome with fits of giggles that thoroughly embarrass us. The ball is where I hear about Silurga.

IN SEARCH OF UNHAPPINESS

A friend who broke up his home.

I. "What worries me is Silurga, my little daughter. Miriam is young and pretty, she won't settle for life on her own . . ." I'm struck by the name.

II. How the name Silurga was composed.

III. My feeling that it's impossible to be happy with a name like that. I'm not making fun, there are psychological reasons.

IV. The parents of my friend Adamantho, who's just ended his own marriage, were called José and Maria, and they were happy. The psychology of parents who give their children extraordinary names. A desire for the exceptional, a unique flair, genius. In actual fact, parents' vanity. The happiness they desire for their children is relative; what they really want is fame: "My daughter is going to be the next Guiomar Novaes."[82]

V. Psychology of the person who bears an extraordinary name. Must unconsciously fall into a tendency to make oneself stand out from the ordinary.

    a. She will frequently succumb to temptation because her name is Silurga—she's not like the other girls.

b. Her amours will be scandalous. But one day she sees a handsome, strong engineering student, a promising young man, named José. Silurga feels ashamed of her name. *Don't tell him my name.* She eventually tells him herself, but José is shocked and retreats.

c. If she goes to college, Silurga will inevitably become a philosopher and a psychoanalyst. She falls into a literary circle, where she'll strike up a very confused companionship with a futurist poet named Taumaturgo. Because the two of them feel exceptional.

d. And if she marries, Silurga will demand equal rights, refuse to have children that deform her body, and one day, she'll never quite know why, she walks out on her husband. She was not destined to be a married woman. Sincerity above all. And yet another home will be broken.

VI. Nobody quite knows why, but the root of this destruction lies in the name Silurga, the name sought out so that she might be exceptional and that marked her out for unhappiness. I can't remember if it's Gide or Huxley who talks about how mankind perfectly organized the lives of domestic animals—coupling up the couples, giving harems to the sultans among them, avoiding both warfare and connubial mismatches. Humans themselves are the only animals that humans haven't been able to get anything right for. They charge down every path to unhappiness and name their children Taumaturgo, Iseo, Miriam, and Silurga instead of Armando, Julio, Paulo, which are so pleasant to say. And because of that, at least in large part, my friend's became yet another broken home. I forgot to say—this friend of mine, his name is Adamantho.

IQUITOS, JUNE 24

The names of a family from the North (the Wanderleys) living in São Carlos (São Paulo):

Brasilianite
Brasilianife
Brasilianisque
Cajubi
Cajuci
Cajudi

And the last one to show up, they called Calobrama.

Father Gustavo, mother Almira—their daughter = Gusmira.

A black woman in Araraquara named her daughter Vanadiol.[83]

And once the war in Europe ended, another in Araraquara
named her son Neutro.

The current mayor of São Carlos, Carlos Simplício Rodrigues da Cunha, who's barely more than illiterate, thought it
pretty when he heard folks talking about the Rua do Ouvidor—
and so he baptized his son Davidor.

In Iquitos I met a Chinese woman named Glória. I've known
only one glory in my life . . . But this one kissed me. Faced with
this sordid Chinese glory, I felt ferociously disconcerted. She
had a name that didn't belong to her, and it was impossible for
me to kiss her back.

THE RAT OF THE SABINES

The first mate on the *São Salvador* once heard that white rats
killed ordinary ones. So he, looking to get rid of the rat race on
board the steamboat, bought four white rats and set them loose
as an experiment. Since he didn't want to get into the business
of breeding white rats, he bought four males. No sooner had
the ship set off than dead rats started piling up—no doubt
about it, the white rats surely were stronger. But after a while,
there came a bunch of brindled rats that took over the whole
boat and were eliminated only with great effort. The thing is,
the white rats really were stronger than the regular ones on all
counts.

A DAY IN IQUITOS

Every time we come off the ship, we're inspected. But here's a terrific story about smuggling. It was June 24 and a steamer was in the port. It occurred to the sailors to put on a boi-bumbá to march through town. They'd soon built an enormous ox, so big it needed two men to carry it. One sailor played Mãe Catirina, another played Cazumbá,[84] and the whole troupe went traipsing down from the ship along the floating pier. The guards, thoroughly entertained, let the group go by with their funny dances,

> Boi Caprichoso won't eat grass no more,
> Cowhand, you'd best do what it wants . . .

and there they went. Well into town, tho, in a shady deal with a Peruvian in some bar, they turned the ox over. It was full of bottles of cachaça and packs of those famous Brazilian cigarettes. They made a bundle.

JUNE 25

I forgot to say: yesterday on an outing we went by the local movie theater, which was advertising, with great fanfare, the last showing of the magnificent film *Do It Now* with William Fairbanks. See, the film had been tagging along on the ship with us . . . Today we set off. Morning visit to the market. Even less interesting, in terms of the goods on display, than the one in Manaus. But the people are a sight to see. On this side of the frontier we often run across pages out of the finest American magazines along the calles and in the forests. Peruvian folk are much prettier than the Amazonian Brazilian sort—there's an undeniable shift that can't be chalked up to nativist pessimism. And they've got no complexes, it's enough to make you jealous. Peru is the best country in the world. At the club, as I perused the interesting drawings in newspapers and magazines from Quito, I was told that the Peruvians make the best drawings in the world. But the best part is the war with Chile—just like '14 Germany. They won and won, and in the end they explode in fits of fury against Chile, all because Chile won the war. I've heard the story about three times now. And these Iquitenses speak with their mouths full of tiny little stones, the delicacy of which is quite debatable and which they spit from their lips in an extraordinarily skillful hurry. They really do speak so quickly that when you start getting hit with the little stones, bam: the sentence is over and you haven't understood half of it. The opposite of Brazilian speech, where by the time you've understood the meaning of the sentence, memorized it even, the molasses jug isn't half done pouring.

At noon Captain Carrillo had the nerve to host a cocktail for Dona Olívia at the Club Iquitos, and of course even I was invited. I didn't go and neither did the girls, something of a scandal. But the best part was yesterday, as we were coming up to Nanay, when Dona Olívia came to ask me not to go out strolling "American-style," in my sports shirt with no jacket. After the official visit yesterday, I went out like that, since I'd seen that all the healthy local Englishmen and Americans did too. But apparently I caused a scandal because I was a visitor, and it was considered a sign of disrespect for the glorious capital of the departamiento of Loreto. Around two o'clock, I went to see the most delightful thing around, the painter Zarela Menacho, in a house with a courtyard, the most beautiful in all Iquitos. Delightful visit. Four o'clock, official farewell visit to the prefect, more speeches. Felt like the Pope receiving the Queen of Belgium. And the consul, oh, the consul! Five o'clock departure, the whole of the government and the whole of Iquitos on the floating dock. And life on board, the steamer full up. The mahogany logs piled up at the bow block the view. Cool and quick as we head downriver. The steamboat seems transformed, seeking out the middle of the river, abandoning the banks in the distance. But the fog stops the ship in the night.

Sun on Peru's face / The sun of Peru on us

JUNE 26

Cloudy sky, rain. We went by San Pablo around lunchtime. Life on board, packed to the gills with people, Brazilians aren't the only ones who travel with all their kids in tow. *"Dame tu mano para que no resbales." "Ya lo creo." "Sírvase usted."*[85] Scales is flirting with an utterly ungainly Englishman, a fellow with his binoculars propped up on his whiskers. We spend the day eating Peruvian coconut candies—there's truly nothing more serious to do, unfortunately. The worst about this full-ship feeling is the horde of invisible people who crowd horribly around. There's no rooftop, no place whatsoever where I don't feel people all around me. At dusk, Leticia, customs. Dr. Vigil bids farewell. Word has it he's a smuggler, which makes him a good deal more interesting. And no sooner have we drifted into Brazilian waters than out pops a Peruvian navy officer, pleased as can be, who'd been hiding out in Hideous Poxie's cabin.

Introductions. And here comes Tabatinga, invisible in the dark night.

JUNE 27

Seems that goodness knows where, way up in the Andes, an Englishman had married a pretty Peruvian woman. Well, it so happened that a Peruvian navy lieutenant, a fairly ugly fellow but with plenty of charm and an easy laugh, cut the line and managed to bedeck the brow of fair Albion. Word got out and the Peruvian lady's brothers, who prided themselves to no end on their alliance with England, backed their brother-in-law with such a vengeance that the Peruvian fellow had to hide out for the first time. Even so, after the whole affair had been dozing toward oblivion about three weeks, he managed to get the Englishman to come alone out to a remote place and asked him if it was true that he and his brothers-in-law were dead set on punishing lieutenants in general for their sensuous indulgences. The Englishman said yes and then the Peruvian navy lieutenant gave him a beating, a stupendous beating that introduced the foreigner to all manner of Peruvian beds, from the chigger-infested ground to a series of hospital cots. Then the English got riled up and bawled so loud the embassy got involved. The lieutenant found himself a wanted man, but he caught such a toboggan of fright that in no time at all he'd slid down from an altitude of three thousand meters to the floodplains of Iquitos, along the Marañón. It was expressly forbidden, but everyone sheltered the little lieutenant, poor thing! and under the green-and-golden wing of Brazil, he hid himself away under the international auspices of some Hideous Poxie or other, then just as soon as Leticia was past he emerged in the dwindling light of night and into all the days to come. And everyone embraced him, which I found quite edifying. And, after all: what is a cuckolded Englishman to the green-and-golden wings of compassion?

Chilly night, and today too. A cold snap has blown down from the Andes like a lieutenant. We Paulistas welcomed it gratefully. While the Amazonians are all woebegone and shivering, we're buzzing with glee. Morning in Esperança. Day in Remate de Males, where again we spotted Richard Barthelmess, who didn't even deign to come on board this time. Trumpet heard that he's the son of an Italian mother and a Peruvian father, born in Brazil. Evening back in Esperança. The ex-bride-and-groom we danced with on the way up came to say goodbye, what charming people! No way to sleep, there are children wailing. Then Scales gets the idea to start crowing like a rooster. Trumpet imitates her, I imitate her, the lieutenant imitates her, and ten-odd people in the cabins build a tremendous artificial chicken coop that, while it may not have brought on the dawn, at least forced the mothers to take better care of their children. Going to sleep. Most laughedest day of the trip.

JUNE 28

The chill is still here. Morning in Santa Rita, where we bought our tucum hammocks. I was stricken with remorse and am now toting, besides my own, two more, one for my brother and one for my friend Pio Lourenço, in Araraquara, who's afflicted with a gentle mania for the etymology of the word Araraquara. São Paulo de Olivença. Stroll with Dolur, talking psychology. Life on board, smelling of children. At night, Tonantins, where Brother Diogo has kept a lamb for us to eat tomorrow. Firewood loaded on. Downriver fast. Departed around eleven P.M.

THE DO-MI-SO INDIANS

I believe that based on the Indians I've come across, whose morality is different from our own, I could write a humorous monograph, a satire of scientific and social expeditions and ethnographies. It would be the tribe of the Do-Mi-So Indians. It may be riper for humorous inventiveness if I say that, instead of speaking with their feet and legs like the ones I saw, during the prehistoric period of the separation of sound into verbal sound with intelligible words and inarticulate musical sound with no intellectual meaning, they went in the opposite direction: they gave intellectual meaning to musical sounds and attributed merely aesthetic value to articulated sounds and words. The name of the tribe, for example, was the two ascending intervals that in our musical system we call Do-Mi-So.

I meet the Do-Mi-So Indians as we come up the Madeira. This avoids a painstaking description of the landscape during the trip upriver—I'll do it as we go downriver, that's quicker. I come across a Paroara singing in third class. We become friends and one day he asks if I want to see something. He tells me to ask the captain to stop just a bit farther on, at the mouth of a stream, and takes me to meet the tribe. Talk about the physiology of these Indians, all of it made up. Describe the tribe's ceremonies, their tribal relationships, family, phratries, etc. Religion. Their philosophy and the way they argue. Their communism. Finally, a series of myths, pure invention on my part. Origin stories are fertile ground for fantasy. If I included vocabulary, that could be quite funny, but only people who know something about music would catch it. And musicians in general can be so dense . . . Better forget the vocabulary.

JUNE 29

Back to monotonies. Balseiro: a floating group of sticks, trees, wood, grass, especially Spanish cedar . . . The chill has gone. We stop at Fonte Boa, as well as other places. A capybara pup in a canoe. Dance on board. Word has it the Peruvian couple dance quite well, they perform two theatrical tangos—absolutely sidesplitting. Then the Peruvians on board dance the marinera. Heel-tapping and handkerchiefs in hand. In my jotter, I find this note: "Fuentes the Peruvian's wife . . . and me." But I can't for the life of me remember what passed between us—nothing bad, there's no forgetting a bad thing. The jotter goes on: "Sleep out of anger."

JUNE 30

Morning in Caiçara, the beautiful lake behind us. Tefé around lunch, the priests' house. What with the prevailing mishmash of races, they asked us to sign the visitors' book and put down our national origins. So and So, Peru; Whatshisname, Syria; Dr. Suchandsuch, Rio Grande do Sul; Schaeffer, Switzerland; Scales, São Paulo; Customs Guard, Amazonas; Mário de Andrade, Brazil. Of all the Brazilians on board, I was somehow inadvertently the only Brazilian. Life on board. Peruvians friendly, Americans too. We spend more time with them: Brazilians are physically and morally awkward. For pity's sake! Once again, I find in the diary: "Fuentes the Peruvian's wife and me." Now, unlike the first time, there's no ellipsis between the two of us. But it was nothing good, I'm sure of that, there's no forgetting a good thing. Plus, in the jotter, I find today's date, at two in the morning, and the following note:

THE IARA[86]

I managed to spot the Iara. She surfaced all of a sudden, luminous, half her body out of the water, taking good care not to show me the fish part. She really is quite pretty, a bit like a certain vamp who'd been ruffling my calm not so long ago, back in São Paulo. A slightly steely profile, short-cut black hair. The crimson of her mouth is vividly defined. Her song is sweet, with a swaying rhythm but no syncopation.

This note proves once and for all that nothing whatsoever, good or bad, happened between me and Fuentes's wife.

JULY 1

Rainy morning. Stop for firewood at São Sebastião. A boat full of soldiery goes by, headed for Coari, where the mayor's been killed.[87] Up ahead Codajás, with bird taxidermist. After a day treading water to satisfy the little wooding stations, at eight

P.M. we arrived at Manacapuru, seen only in our imagination. But raffia hats and baskets came on board, gleaming bright.

To refer to a miser—in São Paulo we used to say "stingy as a dog," but that's long since forgotten—here in the North they say someone's a *munheca de samambaia*: as tightfisted as a fiddlehead fern.

I'm told that the smaller steamers can get through the shallows like this: Since the boats are flat-bottomed, when they spot a sandbar up ahead, they go full speed ahead and ram the little boat into it. The steamer runs aground, but the paddle wheel keeps on spinning hard; the water surges back violently around the boat, picks it up in its arms, and throws it over the other side of the sandbar.

THE DO-MI-SO INDIANS

Alongside the Do-Mi-So tribe, I could make up an inferior tribe, the slaves of the Do-Mi-Sos, all because they spoke using words like us, and this conceptual narrowness made them unutterably inferior. Through this tribe I can make up a whole vocabulary, pure fantasy, with words that are far more sonorous and descriptively, onomatopoeically expressive of their meanings.

I'm strolling through the king's great hut and in one of the chambers I come across a queen eating, the naughtiest thing. She's infuriated and gives me a tongue-lashing. Out came a shower of sounds, trills, staccatos, and octave leaps, at a speed and in a remarkably virtuosic bel canto, my god, what a tarantella!

For that matter, I must note that the number of sounds they possessed was far superior to our poor chromatic scale. Quarter tones were common, with fifth tones here and there. One of the bigwigs in the Do-Mi-So tribe (what if I called them the Mi-Mi? . . .) uttered word after word in which I could make out sixth tones and other aural niceties that struck me as even subtler. He had invented a vocabulary that was entirely his own and that nobody could understand. He was a great philosopher, everyone said so. Those who, after several years of study, were able to decipher him found him a genius and commenced a downward slide that left them completely degraded. I heard the philosopher addressing the people many a time, sitting on the roots of the kapok trees or perched in a hole in a tree trunk. He spoke like the gentle warbling of a little bird; and with the exception of the degraded disciples, everyone would gradually nod off. Then the philosopher would give his head a little shake, and with a forbearing smile understand and accept people's inability to follow along with him. He'd fall silent. And since the work of warbling had filled him up with air, he'd let out a string of melancholy farts.

JULY 2

The small hours found us in Manaus. Mayor. Lunch on land. I escape from school visits. Easy conversation with Raimundo Morais at Ponto Chic. Preparations. Olímpio the doctor furious that he has to come along on the trip along the Madeira on our account. Clóvis Barbosa, writes for *Redenção*, pleasant. Departure at six P.M., Dr. Monteiro, governor, and the rest. Good folks, *gente boa*, Fonte Boa . . . I found Manaus hotter than Iquitos . . . For what it's worth, when it comes to heat, you more or less get used to it. You can't get used to it entirely because of the locals, who unfailingly tell us every single day and all day long that "today is really exceptionally hot." And there began one of the vastest sunsets in the world, impossible to describe. The sun set all across the heavenly vault—north, south, east, west. You couldn't tell which side the sun was going down on, the sky pink and gold from top to toe, then lilac and blue, then black and scarlet raging through. Manaus on our starboard side. The black waters below. It made me feel like crying out, dying of love, forgetting everything. When the pleasure grew so intense I couldn't bear it anymore, my eyes filled with tears.

JULY 3

Dawn found us on the Madeira, at the Santo Antônio wooding station. I forgot to say that we're traveling on another steamer now, the *Vitória*, which rides easier than the *São Salvador*. Captain Jucá, a Mephistophelian butterball, much pleasanter than Hideous Poxie. And the caboclos are so cheery! A much more inhabited river. Nice-looking houses, better than along the Solimões. Now I understand: people always told me that the Madeira was a "happy" river when I got to praising the birdsong on the Solimões. Here there are far fewer birds, but far more folks. And a "happy" river in these vast lands with few people in them means a river with people, not a river where you can hear the birds sing. I'm in quite high spirits again, but after the Caiçara wooding station, wiping the chiggers off me with cachaça in my cabin, I hear the kids on board playing in the saloon. They're dragging chairs around, and one says: "I'm the Amazon River Line!"

Another shouts right away: "I'm the Madeira-Mamoré!"

"Come on, Josafá, you can't be out in front of me! That's Porto Velho!"

They go on like that, and suddenly I'm struck with melancholy. I became a Pullman car on the Paulista line, the railway to Cubatão, coffee plants, telephone: Cidade 5293, a rush of agitated, irritated anguish, wanting to be at home for good, enough with the traveling! That's that, I won't have dinner. I lie down in a sweat. I like knowing that I'm sweating, that it's hot as all get-out, that I can't stand it anymore! And I fall asleep. Around two in the morning we go by Borba, seen in dreams. Terrific nightmare. Rain all night.

LITTLE GIRL

You're sitting down, she comes over and puts a hand on your shoulder.

"Seven more days till we get to Porto Velho."

"What's your name?"

"Magnólia, I'm traveling with the captain. Going to see my auntie."

"Is that girl in the blue your sister?"

"No, my future sister-in-law."

"I see . . ."

She says this in an astonishingly nonchalant, firm way. And she can't be ten years old!

"I'm Bolivian by birth, but I consider myself Brazilian."

"Where do you live?"

"I've been living in Belém for six years. Right after I was born, my mother ran off with another Bolivian. Now she's in Rio de Janeiro with a different Bolivian. She ran off again. She's changed Bolivians about five times now."

That's all right, except the part about her mother being in Rio. Everyone on board knows by now that Magnólia's mother was murdered. One of the children nearby overhears and says: "Your mother's dead!"

Magnólia quivers, caught in a lie. Her little eyes blink fast, and she flushes, terribly ashamed to have a dead mother. But she fights back. She lifts her little face haughtily and asks the boy: "Well, what about yours? Isn't your mother dead yet?"

"Mine's not!"

"Well, my mother's dead!"

There's a moment of stunned silence at the pride with which Magnólia proclaims her mother's death. The children seem indecisive, unsure whether they're feeling envious at not having a dead mother. Magnólia retires, slowly and firmly.

POLITICAL SKILL

In Pará, the Government named as mayors for little towns only people who were from elsewhere, so that the new mayor could take a free interest in the little town, unencumbered by local politics. And indeed, the little towns developed quite well after that. What did the Government do in Amazonas? Instead of naming folks from elsewhere, they named natives who were well situated in the politics of each little town. That way, they loved their native soil, were well situated on it, had an intimate familiarity with local needs, and could work more productively. And indeed, the little towns developed quite well after that. That's what they say.

DONA, SHALL WE SAY, ZEFA

Speaking of governments, I was told about another one, in Amazonas, which came to be known as "the administration of Dona (shall we say) Zefa." They say the governor was quite good and all, that he did want to be honest, etc., but Dona Zefa bossed him around, and she was a good lady too. So her husband, up in the governor's mansion, would get a little note from her:

> Husband dear, the *Hildebrand* is in the port and I hear it'll bring in about a hundred and fifty thousand. Give that to Alarico, but the profit from the *Francis*, which will be over two hundred, goes to our eldest, who needs it more and is about to get married anyway. Kisses from your Zefa.

> The son of a political boss
> No sooner is he made
> The father says, my wife's got
> A soldier on the way
> But before he up and enlists
> I want him getting paid.[88]

JULY 4

Early in the morning, we went by Sapucaia-Oroca. This used to be quite the festive pueblo, they say, and they were in the middle of an outrageous jamboree for the Christ Child's Day, December 25. Well, a good old lady was at the party on account of her daughter and son-in-law, and her little grandbabies came over to her to complain that they were so tired they were about to drop. The old lady said she'd take them home, but before she did, she tried to convince her son-in-law and daughter, it was late, they should come too. She even reminded them that with her old lady's arms—even a good old lady's—she'd have a hard time making it all the way across the wide broad river to get home. But neither her son-in-law nor her daughter paid her any mind, and they threw themselves ferociously into a samba. The old lady shook her head, gathered up her grandbabies, who were all down in the mouth, got into the canoe with them and thought what on earth was she going to do. She wasn't strong enough to row against the current, but what now? The grandbabies crying. So in desperation she took up the jacumã, just like that, and soon as she started rowing she couldn't believe how strong she was! Well, soon as they made it to the middle of the river, a tremendous racket rang out from Sapucaia-Oroca, the old lady turned around, grandbabies too, and the land had fallen. In a split second, in a roar, everything, the houses, the depot, everything was gone, people, music, party, and all, sunk down into the waters of the river. Only the good old lady and her grandbabies were saved. But every year on the Christ Child's Day in Sapucaia-Oroca, you can hear the violin and the guitars from that jamboree playing, haunting the river bottom. In Lagoa Santa, Minas, I heard a story of the same sort about a drowned city.

We stopped at Vista Alegre, the best property on the Madeira, with the church's facade collapsed. Handsome house, excellent. At four-thirty we stopped at América, the trading post on Araras Island, the biggest on the Madeira. We got off. Eight-thirty, São José do Uruá. The girls are a bit lukewarm. Too few Americans on board. At eleven, Vencedor, Carlos Lindoso's depot,[89] a man from Maranhão going on to Manicoré. We'll be loading on firewood until four in the morning—which is when I wake up. On a trip to Iquitos, each of the Amazon River's steamers burns through something like four hundred thousand logs. On the Amazon, a thousand goes for twenty-five mil-réis. On the Solimões, sixty. On the Madeira, around fifty. A sailor on a steamboat, "heavy labor," can't clear two hundred a month, not even with extra pay.

FIBERS AND NOMENCLATURE

Yesterday at the Caiçara wooding station, we bought hats and baskets made of tucumarumã or tucu-maruã-piranga, a reddish palm fiber. I also heard tucumãuã and tucumãhy or tucumã-açu. But another fellow, a major, swore to me that it was actually murumuru and not anumã, "like those folks were saying." But nobody was saying anumã! . . . White tucumã hat. Tucumarumã hat. Carnaúba hat. Timbó-açu hat. Raffia hat. Panama hat.

Sacado: when, at a sharp bend, the river cuts across in a new channel. The old bend, now useless, is called a sacado.

Casquinho de caranguejo: an excellent dish, and quite striking when prepared in the crab's own shell. When a fellow spots a good-looking girl in Pará, he'll say, "So and so's a real casquinho." Since turtle-hunting consists of grabbing one on the beach and turning the critter over so it can't run away, the young bucks say they're going "turtle-tipping" when they head out in search of more or less undressed caboclas on the beach to . . .

JULY 5

Night still yawning wide. The eye of a comet up high, above the bow. Seems it's going to brighten, but then comes a burst of deep darkness. Before any forewarning of brightness in the sky, the river gets to dawning and stretches out in a first aching for color. An unmistakable cold comes on. In the warm swelter, not just damp, downright dripping from the night, there comes breezing round a corner of the river an almost-glacial air that wakes up. It wakes up the first drowses of colors, that's all, no birds yet. A vague, almost-imagined aroma—because the rivers in Amazonia aren't perfumed—a whiff of perfume enchants the air and there's the feeling that the day'll come out from behind the jungle. And then the horizon starts to exist. It's a dark, hard bar, laid down around, surrounding us all the same on all sides. No evaporation. Hemmed in by this ragged horizon, the still-slow water of the Madeira, flowing out hesitantly, held back by the more imposing waters of the Amazon, is still brighter than the sky. To the east, a few tendrils of watery, listless colors laze around. That pesky chill insists on bothering us all, but the day is coming on slowly, watery's the word, almost no color, more a wavering light than a decided color, blackening a few little clouds that have stepped out in front. I swear the first sound to be heard was the rooster of a civilization still slumbering in the hammock of a little palm-straw hut. But an awake ear can sift through the burbling of the cleft waters and the binary huffing of the boilers and make out a few second-rate trills, sighs really. Everything comes on slow. Only the color, when it really comes out, defines itself quickly. A look that darts away from the dawning will find new colors by the time it turns back. The blue settles fast, the color of Our Lady's robes. A pink—washed-out, quavering, malaria-sapped— throws itself into the air and then quietly swoons, turning into a colorless yellow and winding up white. Just enough time to light a cigarette and even the clear blue from a little while ago has whitened too and we've got a disagreeable white sky, with gray clouds farther on. And that's it. But look at that little cloud coming from the east, what's hanging off that tail coming from behind the trees, yes, it does have a hem of bright purple. Not purple anymore, it's scarlet. It's scarlet and the little cloud thrills, stained deep down with shining pink, bloodred, and some gold on the fringes too. Now the whole round horizon gently pinks. The clouds work up courage. From far off, high atop the sky, I see a gaggle of them, all dressed in bright light, perfect oranges and a few blond-headed white ones with a childish air of life. Now the whole river is bright crepe, which the breeze dots with the squawks of three seagulls. And right where that scrap of island ends, the horizon squats off into the distance, and the sun drills down into your sensations. There's a foundry blaze thrusting down into the reflecting waters. The river darkens round, pure gray, a lone living stain, ringed by reflections and the orange gold glare overhead, sublime, violently grand. The big old cloud up front is the only thing still dark in the sky. The rest is lively blue again, and pinks, browns, greens, oranges, yellows. Little babbles of little birds. The quick breeze breathing into everything. The first haze at the mouth of the river branch and the first tremendous rapture at the calm. Scorching day coming on . . . Round about nine o'clock, meanwhile . . . Clothes already damp. The black floor of the rooftop is dripping, drenched with water that didn't rain. And the vivid lines of the kiskadee's cry. Warbling on the low shore to starboard, carried along by the zigzagging branches of the Brazil-nut trees. What becalmed serenity . . . What a world of smooth, fluid waters . . . What a bright mirror . . . The lean-tos by the ports . . . An utter absence of restlessness, of daring, of ambitious Pyrenees . . . And the sun, the sun right there, all white gold, bright, so bright, extraordinarily bright, impossible to stare at. And to think that some folks bad-mouth the Dawn in *Lo Schiavo* . . .[90]

Around eight o'clock, Santa Helena to return a canoe. By afternoon we're in Manicoré, on a high bank, collapsing so fast the line of riverside houses at some parts is just three meters from the crumbling edge. Mayor Feliciano and the judge greet us. I buy cachaça and a carnaúba hat. The outing was the usual crowd, of course, about twenty people behind us, feeling obliged to see everything with us. I was one of the first out front. Then I'm pinched on my leg, inside my gaiters. It's a painful pinch, I rub one leg against another to mask the pain, and ah! all hell breaks loose! Thousands of bites on both legs, pinpricks of fire, I couldn't take it, right in front of the whole troupe I sat down on the ground, yanked off gaiters, socks, rubbed myself, slobbered, screamed, and scampered back to the *Vitória*, an utter wreck. I'd stepped on a swarm of fire ants, never seen anything like it.

To the Golden Lion. "In this establishment no business are [sic] done on Saturdays." I imagined that the golden lyin might dedicate his Saturdays to studying philology, but the local judge, bursting with pride, chimed in that no, he the judge was the one who'd made the golden lyin "fix" the writing on the wall. Something I've been noticing for a long while, the caboclos of the

Madeira have joined the latest fad: fewer kids, more dogs. At just around eight o'clock that night we ran aground for something like twenty minutes. Right afterward we hit a sandbank but didn't run aground.

JULY 6

The *Vitória* smacks into sandbanks and rocks uneasily, giving us a silly feeling of being at sea. Sharp bends in the Madeira. Short stops at Santa Marta and Limoeiro. Around eleven, stop at the mouth of Lake Uruapiara, lots of Brazil-nut trees. We didn't get off. In the afternoon, Bom Futuro, picturesque. The ship's whistle, calling the little canoes over to deliver packages, peoples, letters, the whistles trill until they come back doubled in a string of echoes that rings out all the way to Colombia and the land of the Parecis. Oh, mute shores of the Madeira . . . These beaches don't sing a word, they're too pretty to be smart, just like with women. Flocks of yellow, white butterflies. We're going by the Baianos rocks round six P.M., a tricky stretch for the leadsmen on both sides of the ship. The leadsman: "Three and a half . . . Three and a half . . . Same . . ." And the pilot repeats: "Three and a half . . . Three and a half . . . Same . . ." I finish out my day listening to songs in third class, among pleasant, patient Tapuios.

A HUNK OF PROSE BY WAY OF CEARÁ

A little fellow out of place in third class. Wiry, that good scrawny type where all that's left on the body is muscle. Old Vei, the Sun, sucked all the fat out of him, and in exchange she left burning brown skin and deep-set pale eyes; and whatever was left of his hometown fat was washed away in the rains out near the border with Bolivia, when winter came sweeping over the rubber trees. A winking, half-worn-down air, with a slow voice as he sings over a guitar to see if sleep will come or he can get a hint of a woman, if there's any to be had. Here's what he said:

"I'm going out past Guajará, it'll be three more days on a launch 'fore I get home. Family's in Pará. I just came down to give my mama a kiss. Got a brother in Guajará who owns a launch and another who works at the office in Porto Velho. I've been through this hard life on the river, myself. I sailed for six years, but I gave that up for good. I'll do just about anything, work don't scare me, but it's got to be worth my while. Being a sailor, never sleeping right, hanging your hammock over the cattle, all to make eighty, ninety mil-réis, that ain't for me. I gave it up and stayed in Guajará, working at a German company. Then I bought a rubber-tree stand from the company, the bosses helped out, I bought twenty thousand worth of goods and I set out into the jungle with my men. That year, who'd the Indians up and kill? My backwoodsman. I was left out there in the woods with the harvest and not a clue what to do. Spent the nights scared out of my wits, the Indians trying to burn my rubber, I even up and cried. Without a backwoodsman, you're nothing out there. I can walk in the woods, sure; with my compass I can go just about anywhere, but the backwoodsman's the one who knows, he blazes a trail and zigzags right to where the trees are. That year I lost eight thousand. The bosses forgave four, and I worked off the rest. Now I've got one year left: four years of rubber-tapping's enough! . . . Then I'm selling my stand and going off to Rio de Janeiro."

THE DO-MI-SO INDIANS

Political evolutions and mutations will never produce happiness, no matter how relative. They merely modify the appearance of human unhappiness, the way in which it manifests itself. That is all. And that, incidentally, is enough to burnish their reputation, for they allow the illusion of happiness to remain intact in men's minds.

The Do-Mi-So Indians were organized in a sort of communist matercracy, with a collective distribution of occupations based on the principle of injustice. That way, nobody complained. The mothers were in charge of everything. There were even proverbs about it, initially just stock phrases stemming from the dominance of mothers and women in general. Such as one lively sequence of demisemiquavers, with a downward octave leap at the start. A literal translation would be: "You would go bossy woman deal with." In our tongue, since "bossy woman" is how the Do-Mi-Sos refer to mothers, we might translate it as such: "Go tell it to your mother!" This primitive ritual exclamation, once uttered only by males, meant that they did not feel that the tribe's struggles to feed itself personally concerned them. Now that the utterance has become a proverb, however, it means more or less the same as our "There's more than one way to skin a cat." Its nuances come through in the inflections of the conditional conjugation of the verb *to go*. Indeed, as we saw, the literal translation reveals a conditional *you would go*. This is because these peculiar natives, as I have already noted, have a truly brilliant philosopher among their ranks, who, among other things, managed to prove to many people that movement did not exist. This in turn brought about a violent transformation in the social and intellectual lives of the Do-Mi-So. An exclusively male political party was formed, dedicated to proving that movement did not exist only for men. The women were desolate and began to refer to the men with a falling diminished fifth that means something like "ingrate." At this, the men, with great wailing, met at the Square of the Mother and recognized the need to insert another line into the party's platform, accepting mobility on certain occasions. Rather, since they really could not admit the existence of movement after what the philosopher had said, they changed the word, in their own sounds, to another one that meant "motricity." But ever since then, as they deny the existence of movement, the Do-Mi-So Indians use verbs of movement, motion, and locomotion only in the conditional tense. Currently, any active verb whatsoever is conjugated solely in the conditional—which, one might add, has naturally given them a much more transcendent view of life.

JULY 7

In the morning we went past Juma Beach, beautiful and broad, with a hundred million seagulls on it. There I caught a glimpse of a man who was murdered by the seagulls. He went to grab their eggs and they started diving at him from twenty meters up, pecking him on the head, and the first one that dove killed him. But they're good birds, the pilots say, navigating along the Madeira at its ebb. In the deepdark of night, when the steamer huffs monotonously upstream, the pilot is lulled by the binary juddering of the boilers and drifts off on the job, the treacherous sandbank nears, the ship's about to run around. But then the birds are woken by the noise of the ship coming and raise one hell of an alarm: "Beach here!" "Beach here!" The pilot startles awake, turns the helm, and the ship is saved. At nine we stop at Três Casas, a port without a port, an eight-meter bank you practically have to scale. I got off—that is, I got up there—on my own, since I'd been told that there were Indians around, and famously large bananas too. I saw neither one. All I found was an old man who greeted me pleasantly enough, but the Indians were over somewheres in a distant village, and there was an outbreak of chicken pox. I gave up on the bananas and fled on the spot. At the mouth of a stream, folks were casting lines and pulling fish out of the water through sheer muscular strength. They'd whack the flat of a machete on the fish's head, and farewell, life. River dolphins galore, often two or three jumping out of the water at once, making merry. Ten-thirty, Moanense, I got off. Houses and cows, cows! Life on board. Backgammon:

"C'mon, honey, don't let me down, now! Six and two, six and two, ah . . . six and two!"

"Paris to London!"

"You know I only roll threes, you want to take that risk?"

"Comes down to courage, partner. I sure will."

"Here goes three!"

"Backgammon with a forecast!"

"Man . . . there's times you just feel like grabbing the dice, the board, the stones, your opponent too, and tossing it all in the water! I swear!"

Here, people always talk about tossing things "in the water." Down south, we talk about tossing things "in the trash," "out on the street." It's only natural. Here the kids live their lives in the water, each has his own little boat, they're always wet. Down south, no sooner does her little son get near the wash-basin than the mother takes fright: "Boy, don't you get all wet now!"

I can imagine the mothers up here, with their children play-ing in the dirt, under the sun, yelling out: "Boy, don't you get all dry now!"

At six o'clock, darkness already falling, Humaitá, pitch-black but charming as all get-out. Why on earth are some towns charming and others off-putting? Humaitá is delight-fully charming right away, with a mayor who wears his good-ness on his clothes, and people speaking naturally as could be, acquaintances since the dawn of time. Some part of the local electricity had broken down, and the town was in the dark. We were welcomed in the dark, with people carrying gas lanterns, deliciously between ridiculous and jolly. We were taken over to the "library," where Sérgio Olindense made a speech. Well, we were so used to speeches, the Coffee Queen, the illustrious lady from São Paulo, etc., we weren't paying attention. But no sooner had Sérgio spent a minute on Dona Olívia, there he went: "And you, Mário de Andrade . . ." etc. I was caught off guard. And Sérgio emphatically ticking off my talents, my modernisms and literatures. It's not false modesty, I swear, but I was knocked silly by that speech directed at me . . . I got the impression that this was a tremendous breach of protocol, of the drone of our Amazonian life, I don't know, but it bothered me to no end. And for the first time I didn't repeat my ad lib from Belém. After the speech I went to embrace Sérgio, and since it was plain to see that we were among warm, unaffected, really delightful folks, who wouldn't mind at all, I didn't even make a speech. Then we went to the house of the town's founder, delicious food and drink. They'll put on a boi-bumbá when we come back. The warehouse at Humaitá is an unusual shape. A bright white cement staircase leads from an entry pavilion down to the bottom of the river. For the first time, I saw an ox walking up a flight of stairs. They pushed the poor thing over to the edge of the third-class deck and into the river. The ox goes swimswimswimming around, looking kind of fretful, but folks on the staircase tug on the rope around his horns and lead the swimming ox over to them. And up he goes, as easy as any old fellow.

JULY 8

Whole night at a standstill because of a difficult passage. We only started up again around six o'clock. Well, even then, after half an hour's going, the blade breaks on the starboard propeller. Stop at a beach. But there's no way to fix it here, I don't quite know why. We go on anyway. Mirari (? can't quite make out my note in the jotter) rubber plantation, quite pretty. Around here, the beaches are hosting exhibitions of nighthawks. Moving ahead at a stingily slow pace.

Backgammon:

"One and six, chopping sticks!"

"Two and four, knock at the door!"

"Three and five, man alive!"[91]

Six P.M. We moored in a backwater, with the steamer tied up well, waiting to fix the blade the next day.

THE NIGHTMARE OF THE OTHER DAY

It's nothing special, there's nothing original about it, but it proves that I wasn't made to travel, that I'm fated to live at home among my books, spared from having to deal with lots of strangers. I was in a hotel that had floors upon floors. I was down in the hall, being fearfully attacked, either by a single person (I couldn't make out anyone's face) or by groups of five or six that had teamed up against me. It was extraordinary, what I managed to do in all those brawls: formidable feats, I'd

Pulling the rope to fix the propeller blade

Madeira River. Portrait of my shadow from up on top of the Vitória, July 1927.

Where's the poet?

lash out and I was winning, but I was never able to come out victorious a single time. I would be winning, but I could never arrive at a victory or even my defeat! And this was the terrible torture of the dream. Plus the pain of all my injuries, since the others, even in defeat, managed to land plenty of blows on me too. Then I changed tacks and ran away up the stairs. At this, the torture became even worse. There was an elevator that the staircases wrapped around, but while there was no dreamed-up reason for it, I couldn't take the elevator, I just had to go up all those hundreds of flights of stairs. And each landing brought the same thing: formidable enemies, solo or in groups, and at each landing (now I had a formidable club in one hand) I had to fight and beat them back, I'd knock them all down, took my share of blows too, and then go up and up. Then the torture became downright unbearable, because it occurred to me that when I got to the end of the flights, I'd have to come back down and find all my enemies on foot again, hale and ready to fight some more, I finally let out a scream. I listened hard to make sure nobody had been woken up by my scream—I don't think anyone was. Sweating to beat the band. I put on a robe and walked around the deck a few times, taking the breeze to calm myself down. Took a solid half hour before I was able to lie down and get a decent rest.

JULY 9

Until noon, the sailors working to fix the broken propeller blade. A lovely time playing around on the beach. We leave. Around two o'clock, we went by Calama without stopping, who would ever have thought of not stopping, what steamer would dare not to stop there in the age when rubber was king! . . . Calama once set rubber production records, with the famous rubber-tree stands off the Machado River. And getting off here, not getting off there, we make our way along the bank, Retiro São Francisco, then faraways along the missions of the same name, in the afternoon the Coimbra depot, where I eat good tangerines in the wide vista, and where the guinea fowls, thoroughly backyarded, raise a racket on our behalf. Sometime in the middle of the night, we'll make it to the wooding station Colhereira, where we'll spend the rest of the night. Today we had the strangest sunset, the east all blue and pink. And on a long tongue of sand right in the middle of the river, ducks all in a row watching us go by.

JULY 10

We left Colhereira after day had broken, six-forty. Short stops all morning, what a "happy" river . . . Around lunch we stopped at the Monte Carlos depot, and no sooner had we risen from the table, I got off to see things on my own. The flocks of butterflies, thousands of butterflies, one alone, a watery yellow, is just plain, but the flocks are splendid. Well, when it occurred to me to head back to the steamer, it was a hoot—the *Vitória* was already in the middle of the river, on its way out. I shouted out to Captain Jucá, up in the pilothouse, who was overseeing the maneuver: "What about me, Captain?"

"If you don't mind walking a bit, we're going to stop just up ahead, at Vitória . . ."

"Oh, no, I don't mind!"

I turned to the few folks who were there, soon rustled up a youngun to be my guide, and there I went, through the bright woods along the riverbank, on an Indian path wending through luminous shadows, a sunlit sense of adventure. The little houses all in a row, most of them handsome, cutting down on the kilometer or so that I had to cover. Just up ahead, the big depot— same name as our steamer *Vitória*—the warehouse for all the good rubber from the Jamari. There everyone got off, and a familiar fable unfolded. A Frenchman is traveling with us— well, not with us, he's traveling, and he talked his way into our good graces. We were walking by, the girls, him and me, when we came across a little fellow who'd climbed up a guava tree and was tossing the ripe ones on the ground. The girls wanted some. So I said to the boy: "Not like that, just pick the best ones, and instead of tossing them down, put them in this basket."

And I doffed my hat and made it into a basket of sorts. The little fellow filled the hat up to the edge of my *when*, and when I got it back that full, I couldn't pay him. I handed it to the Frenchman to have my hands free, and while the boy and I settled on a two mil-réis handshake, the Frenchman went off with hat and guavas, offering them to Dona Olívia, the girls, and other acquaintances of his on board, to the delight of all and many effusive thanks. And so it went.

It's so hot . . . The Jamari's mouth gapes on the other side of the river, yawning sluggishly. Afternoon stop at Aliança, where the owner single-handedly opened up a canal to connect his place with the Madeira. The afternoons are increasingly marvelous. Stopped all night because of the difficult Tamanduá crossing.

Chibé: a sort of porridge made from farinha d'água and cold water. Almost liquid, supposedly quite nutritious. On their forced marches, canoe paddlers, the rubber tappers blazing through the backlands, can get by quite nicely on a dish of chibé a day.

JULY 11

The most disagreeable thing . . . Another nightmare tonight, but a different kind. It was just this: suddenly a door opens in my dream, a part of Manuel Bandeira comes into view, and he says, "Telegraph your family immediately."

He closes the door and vanishes, leaving me wide awake with the mother of all anxiety. I couldn't get back to sleep and I can't wait to get to Porto Velho so I can send a telegraph. I know these premonitions of mine, surely nothing's happening at home, they're all well. But it's impossible to avoid the feeling that something bad is going on—a serious illness, death, a terrible disaster. I'm always haunted by premonitions, always awfully violent, physical—so and so has died, this will happen, etc. They never come to pass. People say I should be grateful, but the truth is it's irritating. And now I'm desperate to get to Porto Velho and send off a telegraph.

I leave my cabin, and in the hesitant predawn light the ship braces to try the ill-starred Tamanduá crossing, one of the worst there is. I go up top and Jucá calls me over to the pilot-house. Striking six o'clock. The sun got up at its customary hour, everything's set.

"Shall we?"

The captain just nods. And the *Vitória* slaps its blades in the face of danger and starts moving. The morning, clearly envious of the compliments we'd directed at yesterday's afternoon, is displaying outstandingly poor taste, blending colors willy-nilly. But I can't take a good look, I'm observing the maneuvers. The *Vitória* moves forward gingerly, groping in the treacherous waters. "Two fathoms!"[92] the portside pilot shouted out in alarm. "Two and a half, easy!" consoled the leadsman on starboard. Then the commander turned the helm presto and the ship warded off the imminent disaster. The other bank, not yet pacified, was a pile of rocks with the waves waterfalling off them, drooling with fury, itching to get the ship. "A quarter less two," lamented the portside pilot, and the *Vitória*, swaying hard, nearly came up against the beach on the left, ripe for running aground, a famous turtle breeding ground where years ago you might have tipped over eight to ten thousand of Jupiter's dainties. But the good seagulls spotted this lunacy right away and started up yelling their heads off—"Beach here! Beach here!"—letting us know. "Quarter less two!" the starboard leadsman cried out, "Quarter less two!" threatened portside, and the *Vitória* no longer knew where to turn, and we'd been in this ordeal half an hour, the steamer was going to run aground! But in the end, the false drifting beaches got tired of floating around like that and went down to sleep on the riverbed. "Four fathoms!" the starboard bugle trumpeted. "The ship's rhode it through," says the first mate, Hellenistically.[93] And, indeed, the *Vitória* had ridden through the danger and swam gleefully through this big old world of water.

Around eight, arrival at Porto Velho, with Santo Antônio, on the same bank and belonging to another state entirely, Mato Grosso, half an hour's look away. Official reception. A public school, with the teacher in a marvelous state of chubby elegance, just a lovely thing! going along with Dona Olívia. Heaps of introductions. Visits. Market with no personality. Newspaper. Lunch on board. Finally I can go out more freely. I send a telegraph. Photographs.

"Mr. Mário de Andrade, the secretary to the Coffee Queen."

This time I blew up, I just did! "But . . . I'm not Dona Olívia's secretary!"

"But! . . . didn't you come along with her?"

"Yes . . . we're very good friends."

"So you're taking this trip on your own account!!!"

I couldn't bring myself to get mad at the man, he was too shocked, coming face-to-face with someone who wasn't a drooping, clearly half-crazy queen and who'd chosen to take a jaunt around those parts. Then I explained to him very patiently—a sort of collective explanation, albeit belated, given to hundreds of people who I'd spent time with on this trip—I explained that no, we were a group of friends from São Paulo, curious to see other Brazils, each traveling on his or her own account, all for the vanity or the ecstasy of seeing things.

Afternoon, rail inspection car to Santo Antônio in Mato Grosso. Delightful outing on terra firma, a "state border" marker! in direct contradiction to my ad lib in Belém and elsewhere . . . Walking here and there, calm now, I'd already sent a telegraph, that was all that mattered, enjoying myself. A delightful sweaty outing from which we arrived in great spirits, reduced to dust. The heat is hotter than in Manaus. But I was told here that in Guarujá it's much worse. Altho today is really "exceptionally hot"—it's always the same thing! . . .

I forgot to mention: Today, at the reception, while the ship was still docking, suddenly I heard a train whistle, oh, how I'd missed it! my heart shrank down to a tiny little thing. After all, it'd been more than two months since I'd heard that sublime tenor . . .

SYNTAX

While we were looking for the border marker, I asked the little barefoot boy who was trotting by my side, wearing his eyes out staring at me: "Is it far?"

"Sure ain't."

"You live here?"

"Sure don't."

"So were you born in the state of Amazonas?"

"Sure weren't."

It was exhausting!

JULY 12

Since six o'clock we've been chewing up a procession of dusty stretches, thick in the former "heart of death," each sleeper the body of a fallen man along this, the Madeira-Mamoré line . . .[94] We're going to Guajará-Mirim, São Carlos, Santo Antônio, Jaci Paraná, Abunã. Lunch. The caboclos' pretty little houses, with an adorable sense of architectural inventiveness. And on the long straight stretches, when whirlwinds are born in the void left by the passing train, flocks of frenzied butterflies pour in. I try roselle tea, seen days earlier at a wooding station. Dull and sour, like a piss-soaked kid. I try soursop—and ah, this I like a lot, half wild but amiable, trustworthy and warm, like the Pacanova Indian who comes over laughing, laughing hard, grabs his straw hat from behind and doffs it, raising his arm up high as he holds out the other hand to us in a good-morning, fingers all splayed out. This is Pacanova's first pair of long pants, and he's radiant, the biggest man in the world.

"Now that you're a grown-up, what are you going to be, Pacanova?"

And he, laughing and laughing, says he's going to be a telegraphist, and when we ask why, he says "to marry a Brazilian woman." And then clarifies that he doesn't want to marry an Indian like him, one hundred percent Pacanova is good enough. He wants a Brazilian, one of our mestiças, who's bound to have a little Africa in her blood. The German from the *Vitória* who's come along on the trip and who I can't stand goes and says that Indians are "more Brazilian than the caboclas." I snapped back that Líbero Badaró, Grandpa Taunay the painter, Dom João VI, and Matarazzo were all more Brazilian than me![95] Train plus heat plus a dumb German is more than I can take.

At six P.M. we stopped at Vila Murtinho and ventured over to Bolivia, at the customs post, Villa Bella, qué bella! Flowers, lots of flowerbeds, the feeling of a lust for life, chickens, vegetables . . . Let's get back to Brazil. The train rattles along. And it's me rattling along monotonously on this, one of the ghastliest railways in the world . . . No . . . you can't say it's handsome, no . . . Poor stunted pastures, straggling flooded forests, the still-black swamps running along the waterfalling river and that's it. Nobody's about to find an Athens along the way, no Buenos Aires, either. Nobody, after washing up in the hotel, will be able to go out and see a Burgos Cathedral . . . But these tracks were laid with no kings of Egypt and no slaves . . . No slaves? At least none whipped to death . . . Thousands of Chinamen, Portuguese, Bolivians, Barbadians, Italians, Arabs, Greeks, come in exchange for pounds sterling. All sorts of different noses and skins came round here, lying down with a little fever at dusk and dawning nevermore. What on earth did I come here for! . . .

Today the poet is traveling with his lady friends on the Madeira-Mamoré in a scrubbed-down little inspection car, perched nicely in seats of titica vine, if you'll pardon the name, made strictly by the German from Manaus. A uniformed waiter comes over to bring the poet a cup of Guaraná Simões from Belém, ice-cold, with the most beautiful ice in the world, which comes from Porto Velho. Today the poet will dine on roast turkey prepared by a master cook di primo cartello, who came up on the *Vitória*, deployed by the Amazon River Company to sweeten up our lives. Stops here and there, the landscapes will all be Kodakized, with moving pictures, even! to adorn our future pride with an exotic mud hut, woven together with care and fantasy. And at moonrise the poet has the train wait for him, gets onto a motorboat, ten minutes across the river, and he is born in Bolivia, his homeland. And I smell the fresh flowers of this blessed land, and I hear my compatriots murmuring a gentle tongue, with none of that Peruvian posturing. What on earth did I come here for! . . . Why all these international dead, reborn in the din of the locomotive, who rise up with their dimly gleaming little eyes to spy on me through the windows of the car? . . . This is Guajará-Mirim, just past nine o'clock. Reception. Tired. Not enough rooms for everyone. I nurture an explosive frame of mind. I speak very little, make an effort to be unpleasant, say no to things. I say no to sleeping in someone's house, no, I'll sleep in the train car! No water to wash up. Wash with cachaça. And I sleep in the train car, heroically, no fear of fevers or of the fallen, a furious taste of fraternity on my hands.

JULY 13

Finally they come get me! Excellent wash at the Madeira-Mamoré engineers' house. Morning outing, in which a body's good feeling makes you take photographs unconsciously. Then we go to Puerto Sucre, across the river, a little Bolivian town on the bank. It's ten times smaller than Guajará, but it's exquisite. Every house has its little garden, heaps of flowers, heaps of vegetables, I saw cabbages you wouldn't believe! Bates poured scorn on the people of Amazonas for their unwillingness to surround their homes with vegetable comforts.[96] It seems the presence of the jungle is good enough for them . . . But not here in Bolivia. The head customs officer is a smuggler. Dona Olívia and the Frenchman (who came along just for this) buy beautiful, expensive furs. Expensive out in civilization, that is, here they're dirt cheap. The customs officer sells them himself—and of course lets them through. The outing is delightful and we only get to Guajará close to two o'clock, for lunch. The afternoon outing to the Pacaás Novos fell through. We went around the city again—ugly, truly ugly. A pile of earth-colored, clay-colored houses, no trees in sight, and a handful of pretentious things. The big thing was raising Guajará-Mirim to the status of a city to "be able to raise taxes" and make things easier for some big shots, *uns categorias*, who lived in Cuiabá. Here, *categoria* is used in the masculine—better yet, *catega*. Like the sailor, day before yesterday, boasting to a porter on land: "Madame [*sic*] Penteado is so rich, the biggest *catega* round here couldn't even shine her shoes!"

The city is insipid. Dinner. A common woman wearing a hat, she's got to be Barbadian. But my Barbadian from Belém, she's kept all the charm and loveliness for herself, fifteen days away from here. Dona Olívia and the girls are going to the dance. I refuse so emphatically that Dona Olívia looks at me as if in surprise. Then she smiles. Then she bursts out laughing at me. "Mário, you can acquire your freedom whenever you like . . ."

I disappoint her: "I know, Dona Olívia, but that's not it!"

She smiles a half-ironic "all right" and turns into a capped heron.

Well, but this time really was a bridge too far! I decide to spend my evening at the movies, and they were showing *Do It Now* with William Fairbanks!

Thankfully, the bed at the engineers' house is perfectly soft, and I'm able to sleep without making much of an effort.

NOTICE

In the latrine of the Guaporé Rubber Company.

ATTENTION

The 5 commandments of hygiene, which serve as an easy test of the moral education of those who frequent this latrine, are as follows:

1—neither do your business nor urinate on the lid

2—do not do your business in a squat

3—pull the chain after availing yourself

4—after availing yourself of paper, put it in the can

5—do not dawdle or hold up the rest of the convoy

Hence please observe the commandments above.

(Penciled in below):

6—put Creolin in the latrine on Saturdays!

JULY 14

Set off from Guajará-Mirim, six o'clock. At last we are defini-
tively "heading back." Stop at eleven to visit the Ribeirão waterfall. Splendid outing out over the rocks. Photos. Lunch on
the train. An all-around well-being that comes out in song. I
sing and sing and there's no stopping me. Short stops. We find
the "clock" train, as they say around here too.[97] And a sublime
moonlight descends upon the earth. Everything around the
train has an enchanted light to it, brimming with respect and
mystery. And I sing, I sing everything I know, utterly on my
own. I sing to the moonlight in devil-may-care pure headlong
ecstasy, with the best voice I've ever had in my life, raw but
natural as can be, good, warm, full, wild but with no ulterior
motives, generous. What I feel inside! not even I know! nor
could I, even if I could stop to analyze myself, I'm bursting with
moonlight, I've got moonlight like I've never seen before . . . in
me, in my eyes, my mouth, my sex, my indiscreet hands. The
indiscretion of moonlight, nothing more. I am moonlight! and
suddenly I crouch down, I go all quiet, small, vibrating, vast,
flashing on the inside, not thinking at all, can't think, alone.

   Arrival at Porto Velho, midnight. Slept like a rock.

JULY 15

I get a telegram from home: "All well. Yours, Carlos."[98] In
Guajará it really did seem to be hotter there than here, but it's
only morning and I'm about to contradict myself, it's so hot
out! On board, I jot down the things the sailors write on the
steamers, especially on the hull of the old *Aripuanã*, which is
now in service as a floating dock.

The Rio-Mar
Is the choicest by far
It splits the waves
From Amazonas to Pará

Another:

Cuiabá, the sweetheart of the port.

Well, then a fellow on the *Madeira-Mamoré*, proud of his own ship, wrote, not trying to start a fight:

A man who knows his way
To this will never object:
The *Madeira-Mamoré*
Is a boat you must respect.

Then a brave sailor on the *Curuçá* snaps back, cocksure:

A man who knows his way
Can take the truth on the jaw:
The *Madeira-Mamoré*
Is a cup of coffee for the *Curuçá*.

Delightful to see *coffee* used by folks up north when we say *soup or stew*.[99] But another brave fellow from the *Madeira-Mamoré* struck back in such a fashion that there was nothing left to say:

The *Madeira-Mamoré*
Was what sired the *Curuçá*
It's a strong one, big as kin be
Just like Corporal Corumbá

Corporal Corumbá, they say, was a sort of small-r revolutionary who went around raising heck in the backlands. Funny, the erudite double rhyme in the first three ditties I copied out.

The obligatory visits . . . Candelária Hospital. Festive reception at the Tobias Barreto Day School with the Barão do Solimões School Group, speeches, recitations. I'm given a stupendous jaguar pelt from J. G. Araújo's. We leave just before noon. Life on board. Short stops to pick up rubber, short stops. Now I do find I'm getting a kick out of myself . . . I don't know . . . those twenty minutes on the inspection car, certain specters of the countryside, Santo Antônio, Mato Grosso, an old smell of molasses grass, the sun gone softer in the late afternooning . . . And I hear a little bird from my land, the striped cuckoo.[100] I grew a past again, set my face to the road, and there I went at a steep stride, devouring league after league. The boy had to run, flat out run to keep up with me. Poor panting Captain Garcia kept trying to make something up: "Just look, Dr. Mário! This bridge! The train goes under it!"

As if I'd never seen a bridge with a train going under it! striding on ahead! Finally he couldn't take it anymore, broke into a little run and managed to catch up, taking a firm grip on my arm. I stopped. Then, looking at me very seriously: "There's nothing left to see out there, Dr. Mário!"

We went back to where everyone was. How could I explain to him that I'd suddenly reacquired a past on account of vaguely similar forests and the cry of a striped cuckoo! Brisk walks down farm trails, do-nothing sports under an ever-soft sun . . . The heady smell of molasses grass, and now and then the cry of a striped cuckoo . . .

"There's nothing left to see out there!"

I looked straight out at his "there," the blurred shadows of the late afternoon forest. There was nothing left . . . out there. The smell had gone. The striped cuckoo was quiet. But it was a funny thing. When you, not meaning to, not thinking, just out of nowhere, start walking fast out ahead, not even knowing where you're going . . . Seems downright crazy.

JULY 16

Morning found us at a wooding station, life on board, little stops. We got off at Coimbra, long outing. Scales, Klein, and me. At dusk Humaitá, charming, still no electricity. We went to the home of the family of the town's founder, street lined with tall trees out front, to watch the boi-bumbá. The notes are in my papers on the bumba meu boi. Stupendous night out, under the moonlight and the light of the gas lamps. We set off around midnight.

THE DO-MI-SO INDIANS

Curiously enough, they believed only in evil gods. They had no good deity to speak of. Their mythology was a downright de-monology, perverse as the devil. For that matter, this tribe, for all their good sense, had a concept of goodness that was so thoroughly diluted or lackluster that it, strictly speaking, did not exist. They had all sorts of phrases with subtle musical modifications to designate any sort of negative notion, but for the opposite positive notion, they had, if any, a single generic formulation. For example, I counted up to forty different ways to say, "I am hungry," but they had no way to say, "I am full" or "I am no longer hungry." Now, this was precisely one of the things that made the Do-Mi-So Indians so great—they had made life an ill to be overcome, a demon to be tamed. They were, deep down, albeit an utterly theoretical deep down, a bunch of discontents. And this gave them, alongside all their tremendously progressive activity, an unshakable sense of res-ignation.

To grasp just how delicate this pessimistic view of existence was, one need look no further than a word that begins on a lower tone and slides up to a fifth higher. I noticed straight-away, during the first few hours, that this melody was repeated constantly, and when I asked about it, they told me it meant enemy. I was dumbfounded at this, realizing that this was the melody they addressed one another with, and put my questions to the interpreter. He, poor thing, didn't know much at all and started insisting that the phrase in question surely did mean enemy. But the philosopher, who was standing by listening patiently, broke into a gentle warble and the interpreter listened, listened, and cleared it all up for me. The thing is, in the Do-Mi-So language, the intensity of the sound—the fortes, the pianos, the crescendos, and the decrescendos—did not merely vary the meaning of expressions, they could modify them completely. Not fundamentally, however. And this was the case with the word at hand. The Do-Mi-Sos had no word for friend, companion, boss, owner, slave—nothing of the sort. They really had only a single word to designate the interrelations between human beings of the same sex and not of the same family, and this was that meaning enemy. But if it were spoken in fortissimo, for example, while it still fundamentally meant enemy, the word took on a conceptual air of boss, while in pianissimo it would mean friend, all while retaining the primary sense of enemy. From the start, when I began paying attention to that bit of semantics, I noticed they all referred to me with a decrescendoing mezzo-forte that meant, more or less, "peculiar enemy of an inferior race, hence worthy of scorn." But by the end of our relations nearly all of them, with the exception of about four or five, addressed me in a rising pianissimo, which I could not help but be touched by.

JULY 17

Life on board. Morning found us in Três Casas, but I didn't get off, since I only came out of my cabin after the dinghy had gone. In Pariri we met *Índio do Brasil*, the Amazon River Line steamer, come from Belém. I'm a bit on edge . . . Little stops, I don't get off. For pity's sake! Suddenly I've realized that what with this business of traveling with women, I haven't seen any of the most useful things I could see around here, all on account of this endless train-bearing . . . For example, I still haven't visited a rubber plantation! I go complain to Captain Jucá, who thinks aplenty and promises me a long visit to an

interesting rubber plantation the following day. Thank good-
ness. Around five o'clock, the mouth of the Uruapiara, didn't
get off. Another consummate case of nirvanizing malaria.
From way down the stream, a big boat came along, steered by
two Tapuios, piled high with lumps of rubber. At the bow, looking up at the *Vitória*, is a fellow, how old? no telling, smooth
skin, well shaven, fine lips, just a crease of a mouth, deep-set
eyes, heavy gray circles under them, and a dull gaze seeing nothing whatsoever, slightly paler than the dark circles. Washed-out
fine hair falling straight down. White shoes with no socks.
Clothes as clean as could be, as ironed as could be, S-120
linen,[101] only trousers and a jacket over his skin. Everyone at the
railing, of course, looking out at the boat and talking about it,
a young fellow living in the back of beyond in a rubber plantation. It's entertaining. The first mate explains to us that he's
very rich, his parents are dead of malaria or something, and he
lives on his own in the rubber plantation.
"Married?"
"A bachelor."
The girls raise a ruckus, desiring his desire, the perverse
things. The fellow doesn't even look. He jumps on board, goes
by us without looking, and heads to the commander's cabin to
see to his accounts. When he gets off, he goes around the other
side of the ship, avoiding our gaze. He gets onto his boat and
stands there in the bow. And the boat goes off, turning its back
on us forever and ever. Without one look! It's not a problem of
hap- or unhappiness . . . I can't even really imagine what the
problem is, but it exists, it's real, I saw it with my own eyes. It
may be a matter of problem substitution, watering down prob-
lems with indifference. Or with patience. Or with monotony,
which is more straightforward. It's nearly seven o'clock, and
we've thrilled to the ship's passing through the terribly difficult
(so they say) Marmelos shallows. I can't shake the image of the
young fellow. To have a malaria like that, one that left me utterly indifferent . . .

ANECDOTE

I won't say where it was. We were coming up on a little town. Dona Olívia by my side, leaning up on the railing, alongside other people, watching the town draw near. At this, Dona Olívia sighed audibly.

"What's the matter, Queen? Why the sigh?"

"Ah, Mário . . ." (with a wearied air) "this business of every mayor feeling obliged to go around with us, take us to the town hall, to the school . . ."

Well, that town we visited sans mayor, free, strolling as we pleased. All because the mayor was the very same man who was standing beside Dona Olívia on the ship as we approached, pointing out the church there, the town hall over there, etc.

JULY 18

Around eight o'clock we arrived back at Vencedor, and Captain Jucá sent word that if I was really set on it, I could go into the rubber plantation, since he was going to load up on firewood and could wait for us as long as we wanted. Dona Olívia shied away from the excursion, which promised to be long. I went with the two girls and Klein, guided by a backwoodsman, Eduardo. We follow along a rubber tapper's trail, zigzagging through the forest from one rubber tree to another. We also skirt gigantic Brazil-nut trees—finally, a genuine "civilized" Amazonian forest. The tapper's trail is free of the tangles of vines, the thick undergrowth that we could never hope to penetrate. We eventually catch up to the man whose daily route we were following. We watch him at his work, making slashes in the tree, putting out the little cups, setting out for the next-up rubber tree. At the end of his trail, he'll retrace the same zigzag, gathering the full cups. Another hour of walking and we come to a deep little lake. There's no imagining the feeling of peace, the almost absurd silence of these small lakes surrounded by colossal trees. Here, the feeling is even more intense than in the place near Manaus. And here there are no water lilies, nothing to bring even the thinnest veneer of joy to this impervious tranquility. Even the girls lowered their voices. The water reflects the black green of these huge trees; there's something untrustworthy about its depths, as if it were slowly rotting. And there's a sickly edge to the silence, tho no sadness. Amidst all this, a note that's more bitter than it is funny. A little straw hut on a steep sliver of beach, slumping down into the lake. Nearby the house, dragging herself from task to task, is a woman of about fifty, certainly no less. She's a paralytic and her name is Bernardina. When the girls ask her age, she says she's just twenty-nine.

"And you live alone!"

"Nawww . . ."

"Are you married?"

"Sure am . . ." (and then, lazily): "I mean, coupled up."

The words fall into the water, dead. They sink. We decide to head back, but the walk doesn't cheer up easily; only a quarter of an hour later are we happy again, laughing and talking loudly. All things considered, one of the finest outings on the trip, almost three hours long.

Around two in the afternoon, stop at the São José depot. It belongs to the same man as the one at Vencedor, Carlos Lindoso, who offers me the pelt of a collared anteater—a tamanduá-mambira, or nembira, or tamanduá-colete. This is the prettiest piece of Amazonian forest we've seen yet. We get off. Chitchat about the chances of us, with no guide, getting lost in the jungle. Scales, Klein, and I, tho accompanied by a Tapuio, decide to try. We take all our intellectual bearings and go into the forest. Not a single unique feature escapes us— fallen trunks, a parasitic plant, this, that. No sooner have we walked for ten minutes and decided to head back, confusion sets in. Where's the trunk? Where's that flower? Which way is the river? Only with the sun's help do we straighten ourselves out toward the riverbank and make it there. Where's the *Vitória*? upriver? downriver? . . . Thank you, Tapuio. Life on board, little stops. Sublime afternoon. Cool evening.

THE DO-MI-SO INDIANS

Myth of the Appearance of Man. So it was that the Indians took me to see their giant embaúba tree. It was truly a prodigious thing. In the middle of the dense undergrowth, which was itself a good deal taller than a man, the colossal trunks of that truly virgin forest flung themselves furiously upward, trunks that seven people holding hands could hardly embrace the half of. Well, all that was tiny, the undergrowth was blades of grass, the trunks were rosebushes next to the giant embaúba. I measured its height: over seven hundred meters tall. And then the Indians told me that it was in the vast crown of this embaúba that the howlers and the sloths had their famous fight, nobody ever found out why. One fine day they just got at one another's throats in a terrific free-for-all, and there were as many deaths as there were leaves on the embaúba. A new soil was laid down over leagues and leagues, mounds and mountains of corpses embracing in the forced peace of death. I found it odd that there should have been a war, such an active pastime, in which sloths were involved, but the Do-Mi-Sos just laughed. The truth is, there's been a great deal of exaggeration when it comes to the sloths' sloth—it's all slander, really. Some sloths are really quite rushed even. What's actually going on with these sacred animals is a much more intimate understanding of life and the relativity of hustling and bustling. This being the reason why they are so sluggish. For the Do-Mi-So exegetes, only one question remained. Some, a minority belonging to the animalist school of thought, believed that the sloths' slowness derived from the fact that these animals operate with their thoughts on the future, caring less for themselves than for their children and their race. Meanwhile, those of the school that our scientific knowledge might deem "totemic" swore that it was nothing of the sort, that the sloths weren't concerned with any future whatsoever. Rather, they had merely risen to that level of wisdom at which one recognizes that happiness is not the enjoyment of the pleasures of the world, but rather the full, absolute consciousness of movement. And indeed, I believe nobody will dispute that sloths move with great consciousness.

Each movement they make can last seven hours, as I have observed on many occasions, but is undertaken with a deep intensity—an act of verticality, as the saying goes nowadays. The gesture is, as one might say in sermo vulgaris, "enjoyful." I immediately adopted the exegesis of the totemic school and adhered to the majority, which pleased me to no end. And when I told them that the sloths were also practicing one of the doctrines of a great philosopher of my land, Machado de Assis, who said that "even pain has its pleasures," the Indians started belly laughing in their own way, letting out terrifically high fermatas that meant "That's it!," "That's just it!"

And it is precisely because they base their whole lives on the essential principle of the consciousness of movement that sloths are so happy and good-tempered, and why, in the war with the howler monkeys, they received the palms of victory. Then they divided the world up. They forced the howlers to stay on the ground, while they, the sloths, would take the branches of the embaúba. The Do-Mi-So Indians say they descended from the sloths, while the howlers, forced to walk around on land, gradually transformed into other Indians, and into me. And when I asked how it was that they had descended from the sloths if the sloths didn't have to walk on land, the Do-Mi-Sos were quite struck at the question and answered that they didn't know.

JULY 19

The small hours found us in Borba, the silhouette of which, up on the riverbank, I saw in dreams. Then Caiçara. Last afternoon on this river, hot but lovely. And a miracle: a hard breeze came breezing in, filling me with longed-for pleasures, the smell of a forest in flower, a wild smell, warm, luscious. And night falls. On this trip along the Madeira, I've gotten quite into the after-dinner habit of going down to third class to talk. "Don't know what ever happened to him . . . Once I saw him in Pará, in a shirt and tie, all formalized-like."

"But do you . . . prefer Espírito Santo or Acre, then?"

"Don't rightly know!" A gentle smile. Why'd he go to Acre? I knew it, all to get back at his brother. He really didn't have a head for books, so his brother, already two years into secondary school, said the only thing he'd be good for was tapping rubber out in Acre. Out of pure spite, he agreed ("I had no idea . . .") and ran away from home to go tap rubber in Acre. He had to hide as he went because his picture was in the paper, he even knocked out a front tooth to make the disguise better, went to Minas and from there to Bahia, doing all sorts of work. He spent five years like that, but never a thought of going home! And all of a sudden he was twenty-one, with no papers, no nothing. But he wanted to set sail, to get out to Acre. Finally he set off, working on a boat. In Fortaleza he met a fellow who was headed for Amazonas and felt the itch again. He had a job, but he dropped it, and all of a sudden he had no papers. In the end he was able to get fake papers from a friendly priest, all so he wouldn't bring shame to his parents, down there in Espírito Santo. He even (pulling out a wallet that wasn't even a wallet anymore, it was so old), he even kept a letter he'd gotten from the priest when he was in Manaus. Then he got hired to work on a rubber plantation in Acre, and when he got out there and set foot on land, "I felt proud, yessir." Parents, got none: who'd want to be his parent now! He was thirty-five already, yessir. Espírito Santo, he could hardly remember anymore. Acre, well, you know how it is, sir . . . And in the silence between us two, I heard Trumpet's lovely voice, singing up high on the deck.

JULY 20

Manaus around ten, fantastically hot. No: it really is hotter here than in Porto Velho. But we have to wait until one, permission to disembark. Finally out on the street, shopping. Visit to the governor in his mansion. From there, we set off in dustmobiles, thirty kilometers, to inaugurate the Olívia Penteado Station on the highway that will lead to Rio Branco.[102] Tapuias in scarlet, the national color for country women. Suddenly I'm kissed right on the mouth by a São Paulo–smelling whiff of

molasses grass. The toucans boo us with two-kilometer gales
of laughter. Dinner with the governor and the mayor, at the
best restaurant. Very good. I'll miss these turtle fillets. Visit to
the theater, aggressive combination of false luxury and sloppy
finishing. Handsome furniture in the governor's box. Night out
with Raimundo Morais and Da Costa e Silva. I sleep, having
paid my dues to myself.

JULY 21

I get up bright and early to go buy jaguar pelts. At ten, visit to
City Hall, then to the demonstration field to see the "rational"
way of cutting rubber, with the fabulous Amazon knife.[103]
Lovely, the rubber trees' new leaves! they come out silvery.
Lunch at the Rio Negro mansion. Frankly, this Baré[104] hospitality is extraordinarily courteous, extraordinarily generous,
extraordinarily agreeable. Afterward, a delightful outing and
respective snack at the Tarumã forest and waterfall. Chevalier
came along. And the sharp little fellow from Minas, what was
his name! . . . Finally, on board. Visits, visits, visits to say goodbye. We set off at eight. Well, now we are indeed heading back
to São Paulo. Any step we take in our travels from here on out
will bring us closer to São Paulo. I say this, incidentally, with
no pleasure. I'm not psychologically cut out to be a tourist, I'm
sure of that by now, but I've found myself missing São Paulo
and my folks only about three times now. I've never known
how to miss things, this must be a flaw of mine . . . Terrible
night, I can't get to sleep, agitated, anxious.

THE DO-MI-SO INDIANS

It is curious to note how, even with such vastly different no-
tions of existence as ours and these Do-Mi-So Indians', certain
forms coincide. These Indians too dress themselves up with
flowers and cultivate great gardens tended by the wisest of gar-
deners. The women, who have always been much more sexual

than the men, adorn themselves to draw the males' attention to
their most scandalous parts—which, as we already know, are the
face and head. And so they festoon their necks with water lilies
and water lettuce. There was even a time when they started a
fad of decorating their heads outright, albeit while still covered.
But there was such an outcry, the men themselves felt repelled
by their utter lack of shame. And the fad came to an end—
altho not before the public devouring of some four or five daring flowery-headed ladies who had decided to defy public
opinion. The others soon resigned themselves, reserving the
right to prettify their necks. The young men, however, flowered
themselves up without the slightest hint of sexuality. They were
partial to a kind of purple and yellow-speckled lily that grew at
the edges of the marshes, one with a very slender long stem.
They would cut the flower, stem and all, and stick it in their . . .
in their rear—which gave them something of a brooding air.

JULY 22

Itacoatiara early in the morning. Dona Olívia doesn't want to
be woken and I don't even think of the girls. I get off with the
affable mayor and the journalist from Pará. Out for a drive! A
present of nuts. Around three o'clock, Silves, with the peculiar
ruins of the church, now home to all the dogs in the world.
Pretty girls in the windows. A wind kicks up and the ship starts
rolling. Drizzle. At nightfall, Urucará. The ship rolls. I play
backgammon with Dona Olívia. These Germans are a naive
bunch. The girls, Trumpet in particular, are taking all sorts of
liberties with Klein. Trumpet has already gone to bed. Meanwhile Scales heads over to their cabin, talking with Klein. She
goes into the cabin and leaves the door open. Klein sits down
nearby and keeps on talking with the both of them. All this
through the cabin door that opens onto their inner room. Dona
Olívia there, playing with me. She starts shifting in her chair all
bothered. She shoots a few glances at Klein, no longer hiding
her irritation. He's got no idea. Me, just funning. Finally Dona
Olívia can't take it anymore and gets up. She goes over to the

girls' cabin, asks for a bottle of I don't know what, and ostenta-
tiously shuts the cabin door, looking straight at Klein. But the
big galoot doesn't entendre a thing. The little gramophone is
right there on the table. Klein puts the machine to work. Trumpet's face pops up, just her face, at the part of the cabin wall
that's just netting. She's clearly climbed up on the bed, to have
her face up that high. And Klein chats with her. Dona Olívia is
making preposterous mistakes at backgammon: two plus two
is thirty-five. But now Klein goes over to the girls' cabin and
knocks on the door, calling for Scales. Dona Olívia can't take
it anymore: she gets up, stops the gramophone roughly, and,
quivering with rage, hollers at the German: *"Elles n'ont plus
besoin de musique, Mr.! Elles sont allées se coucher!"*[105]

Trumpet vanishes. Scales, not a peep. They'll be laughing in
there, I bet. I don't know what to move—my left index finger?
Poor Klein has his eyes glazed over, completely rattled in the
wake of that incomprehensible French. Dona Olívia standing
there next to the backgammon board, moving the stones every
which way.

JULY 22

Insert a digression on the "moral" and hence physiological se-
curity of the actions of Musset, Klein, and the Swiss Schaeffer
on the way up to Iquitos. One gets the feeling that they're
backed by a multimillennial tradition that allows them to act
"painlessly," as opposed to the girls' and my moral dithering.
Even the Americans in Iquitos, so secure, having a "civilization" to back them up. Us and this indecisiveness, this inability,
nothing that a tacked-on "ability," a religion of any sort, can
ward off. Hence the permanent pain, the perennial misfortune
of staring down pure chance out ahead. Say that I remembered
a communist Jewish friend of mine who left me *criblé de lettres*
about her social misery, the workers, etc. It occurred to me to
write her an Amazonian letter telling her about this individu-
ally felt South American "pain." Yes, they suffer theoretical
and social pains, but you have no idea how this niggling little

pain, the inability of the moral being to really do anything, awes me and lays me low. And finish up the letter.[106]

JULY 23

Parintins in the small hours, seen in dreams. At five, we stop to take on firewood at Desaperta. We get into a rowboat and go down to Joseaçu Lake (lovely hybridism)[107] to visit Vitória, a pau-rosa oil distillery—it's used as a perfume fixative—owned by a Frenchman of course, Ernest Hauradou. Wonderful outing. The morning is so bright that I take excellent photographs even before six o'clock! The little Frenchman is a linguistic delight:

"Me, I was bitten by a *jararaque*, but I didn't get scared, I didn't do anything. Well, if I'd had a *canivète*, *enton* I would have cut it, but I didn't even have a *canivète*!"[108]

He offers us some pau-rosa oil—the smell is nice, a bit sickly.

Life on board again. We've agreed to get Klein drunk, and an hour before lunch, the Frenchman on board—whose name is Musset, incidentally—invites Klein, the girls, and me to have a whiskey. Terrific spree. Out of practice drinking (we'd been avoiding alcohol on board) and worn out by the heat, I know that four shots was enough to demolish me, leaving me completely drunk. I'd spared the girls. Klein and Musset are quite tipsy as well, but they disappear. Me, out of control, rather than fleeing from the lunch bell, no: I take my seat across from Dona Olívia and to the left of the commander. What's more, the girls, next to Dona Olívia, are making faces and watching me. Aware that I am very drunk, I decide, as I always do, to prove to everyone that I am not drunk, and compliment the first dish. I address myself quite seriously to the commander— I've never been more serious or more circumspect in all my life—and pose questions about the tonnage of the Amazon River Line steamers. Dona Olívia looks at me, a bit uneasy, not sure what exactly is going on. I recognize that I am talking about things that may not interest her and convey to the commander and to the other northerners at the table our ardent desire that Amazonia may rise up in short order and soon rejoin the march of progress alongside the other states in the federation. Dona Olívia is stupefied. The girls, boring holes in their plates with their noses, can't move or they'll explode. Captain Jucá is bewildered. The doctor tries to paper it over, says I don't know what, which leads me to seize on the issue and propose the large-scale industrialization of "oleaginous seeds," because Germany . . . Then Dona Olívia laughs. She laughs hard, she's understood everything, and the girls explode. Commander Jucá grins. I, what am I to do! I laugh. And I am now comfortably drunk. Illustrious sleep. The girls wake me up in the early evening, as we're arriving in Óbidos. I buy an enormous snakeskin. There's a mayor. Stop at the Fazenda Imperial, nearby, to take on two oxen. And, as I am perfectly in accordance with myself, I sleep like an angel.

JULY 24

In the night we went by Alenquer, seen in dreams. Morning finds us in Barreira do Tapará, taking on firewood. A little fellow, a clever Tapuio carrying logs, plays around and laughs more than anyone. I tease him. He smiles, but doesn't answer. He brings more logs. I tease him. Smile, no answer. Brings more logs. I tease him, no answer. But when he gets off the ship to go fetch more logs, he turns and looks straight at me.

"Mister! Wanna take me to Belém!"

There's desire and anguish in the request. Now I'm the one smiling with no answer. I get off. The work is done. I go over to the boy and strike up a conversation. I think of giving him a few nickels by way of consolation.

"Do you know how to read?"

"Sure don't!"

"And would you like to learn?"

"Oh . . . more than money!"

I couldn't bring myself to give the consolation nickels. I went

back on board with my heart pinched. Only after the steamer
had left did I think that I should have given him the nickels. As
consolation, at the very least! Eleven and plenty, Santarém in
the sun. Buying gourd bowls. Scales offers one of them to me,
ironically. It says: "I dreamed of you as I traveled." With the
melody to "Rose Marie," it becomes a song:

> I dreamed of you as I traveled
> Among the pirarucus,
> The ja-carés, the ja-camins, and the ja-cus,
> Cajás, maracajás, and tracajás . . .[109]

We photoed the tame margay. Life on board. In the afternoon,
thrilling entrance to the river branch at Monte Alegre and the
Gurupatuba River. The passage is so narrow that tree branches
splinter against the ship. There's no mayor in Monte Alegre. But
there is rain, and Miz Marta, who learns my name and won't
stop singing it, just like the Do-Mi-So Indians, who aren't interesting me that much anymore. I'm giving up on writing that
book. I buy a timbó-açu hat. Drifting.

JULY 25

If nothing else happened yesterday, I'd have had my day made
by the ponderation of a Tapuioish fellow, getting on in years,
but wealthy and a regular in Belém. We were gathered round
the refreshments table, everyone except the Queen, and the
girls started in with dangerously suggestive jokes, some outright
spicy. The fellow sitting over there, real quiet. At this, someone, I don't remember who, probably the journalist, yes, it was
him, I remember, half threatened with a laugh: "Butterflies to
the light, see you don't get burned!"

    That's when the old man said, calm as could be: "But they
don't get burned, see. They did when the light came from fire,
but nowadays not even light burns, it's all electricity. Butterflies
bump up against the light and keep on living 'longside all the
rest."

I tried to play it straight, but dying to write his name down here, after a while I asked.

He looked at me warily, got up, and said as he left, "Son, I'm a man of the three twenties: twenty a bachelor, twenty married, twenty a widower."

Six o'clock, Almeirim, I don't get off. I get ready to get off at Arumanduba, which is coming up—a formidable property, worth a million dollars gold, they say. Dona Olívia doesn't want to get off and the girls have lost interest in the trip, I don't even ask them along. I get off alone and visit the whole property with Manuel Pinto Nemo, the brother-in-law of José Júlio de Andrade, the senator. Arumanduba is the center. Jari and Cajari, biggest producers of rubber and nuts. Paru, nuts and balata gum. In the distance, leagues beyond, the horizon is endless nut trees. Mountains of Brazil nuts, carpets of balata gum to carpet the whole ocean, heaps of rubber sprouting from the lakeside warehouses . . . Arumanduba with five big steamers, sailing for her and her alone . . . The big boss with a vast netted house on the farm, a house in Belém, a house in Rio de Janeiro . . . Herds of disgusting buffaloes, those horned pigs . . .

The steamer is setting off. Someone hasn't noticed the maneuvering and is still on board. Folks perched up in the warehouse poke fun: "Go on and jump in, Baltazar!"

"Have a nice trip, Baltazar!"

"Give my regards to my sweethearts in Belém, Baltazar!"

You had to hear the belly laughs coming from the warehouse. Finally someone hops into a little boat and comes over to help Baltazar.

Mr. Nemo gave me two handsome howler monkey skins, male and female. And a little crate of nuts to hand out. At two o'clock, Gurupá. Visit to the old fort, church, intendant's office in ruins. Seven o'clock quick storm, masterful entrance into the Straits of Breves, complete with drama and tragedy. Soon after, stop at Arraiolos, nothing but Portuguese names here, to take on firewood.

JULY 26

The *Vitória* makes little stops all night, embracing acquaintances. Laughing, carryings-on, botherating our rest. In the morning, still the Straits of Breves. Pack bags before arrival in Belém tomorrow. In the afternoon, Cocal, a wooding station with raffia baskets and hats. At seven o'clock, Jararaca, an important farm on the Jararaca Channel. Heavy downpour. We left only late at night, once the rain had stopped.

I forgot to mention. Here, steamers are like streetcars, picking folks up at one rubber plantation and dropping them off at the next, and so on. Soon after we'd left Porto Velho, heading back, people came to ask Dona Olívia if she'd really agreed to pay a ticket to Manaus for the woman in third class. What's this now? When they went to take the ticket from a new passenger in third, an old lady, she replied ever so calmly: "The Coffee Queen's paying."

Dona Olívia didn't know the first thing about it but paid up, of course.

JULY 27

Morning finds us sailing through the dingy air of Marajó Bay, an immense stretch creating all the horizons its heart desires. Belém around one P.M. The joy of Belém. But it is . . . exceptionally hot. Automobile over to Souza to pick up the tortoiseshell pieces I ordered from Antônio do Rosário. To my great credit, my ink blotter, which I sketched out and provided the proportions for, is the loveliest I've ever seen. Afternoon on the terrace of the Grande Hotel, truly marvelous state of well-being . . . Another bath, then dinner. My lady companions go to the movies, where *Do It Now* is no longer playing. I let myself linger on these broad sidewalks, sipping up a cold guaraná and Clóvis Barbosa's ohsochatty conversation.

VARIANT

The myth or anecdote about the priest and the game of "I want you to go and come back and bring me such and such" has an anticlerical variant. Father Julião, they say, when they were building the Hospital da Beneficência Portuguesa, used that game to take things out of the hospital and build his own house . . .

BELÉM—ST. THOMAS AND ALLIGATOR

On today's visit to the Goeldi Museum, the director, who was accompanying us, treated us to the spectacle that is the black alligator's lunch. What an angelic lunge! . . .

The monstruous critter was stock-still, keeping an eye on us, halfasleep. The worker tossed a duck a good half meter over the water, and the gator just went chomp! It snapped the duck up and sank back down into the shallow tank. Through the clear water you could plainly see the duck sticking out of its green maw. Neither alligator nor duck was moving. There was no gush of blood, no cry, no ferocity. It was a simple chomp, and "the Spirit of God moved upon the face of the waters once more."

The alligator's lunge left me in a sincere state of religiosity. I give you my word, I felt God in that lunge. The speed! The incommensurable eternity in that gesture! and, above all, the impossibility of error! Nobody misses a lunge like that, and, indeed, there was the duck, no cry, no blood, I do believe with no suffering, there in the critter's mouth. A great surprise and a swoon, from which it passed into death unknowingly. And from death to the alligator's belly.

And the black alligator there, so quiet, all long and pure with its sweet eyes, had the air of an angel. Now, don't think I'd go so far as to populate the heavenly homestead with winged alligators. This wasn't a true similarity, but rather an air: the alligator had the air of an angel. In that chomp, so swift as to be invisible, I detected that immediate knowledge, that metaphysical intellection, which St. Thomas attributed to the angels. Ah, humanity, the superiority of irrational beings over us rests in this, the wholly angeliform integrity of their knowledge. It's easy enough to say: alligator intuited duck and thus ate duck. That's all well and good, but within ourselves, we divide up the sensation, the abstraction, the consciousness, and then the will that desires, or does not desire, and finally acts. We lack that absolute immediacy that the alligator possesses, and which angelifies it. You might say it slipped out of time in that terrible chomp. See duck, know duck, desire duck, snap up duck, it was all one. The chomp wasn't even a reflex, it was truly simultaneous, part of the knowledge itself. That was what helped me see the angel in the black alligator.

A quarter of an hour went by that way. Then, with two or three jerks in a row, the alligator adjusted the food in its maw to begin its lunch. The water pinked a little—it was blood. That brought me back to that connection with the Divine prompted by the lunge. I felt a need to settle into reality myself, and, since we were at the Goeldi Museum, I went to examine the Marajoara pottery.

Our earthly revenge is that the alligator, with all its extemporaneous intuition, hadn't had a bit of pleasure. When the water started pinking, that's when it might have tasted a bit of its food. Tasted duck. A taste of duck, like when you open up your eyes and spy a whole mess of colorful pots. You say, "How pretty!" with the same inevitability that the black alligator . . . just knew "duck"—and chomp. With the same inevitability, but not in the same way, tho. Human rationality has allowed us to distinguish, within time and with acquired knowledge, and to put a name to the prettiness of Marajoara ceramics. But that prettiness will be different for each of us, and for each distinct and splendiferous. The alligator will never truly enjoy duck in this life. What for us is Truth, variegated and slippery Truth, for it will never be more than Essentiality, always the same irreducible essence. Alligators lack the principle of contradiction, and they will be, eternally and inescapably, pantheists. Only we feel not just the taste but also the joy of blood on our tongues. And the pleasure of life begins.

JULY 28

Belém lovely as can be, the best thing in the world, market and Rua João Alfredo (the local Quinze de Novembro) all morning, shopping and messing around. Day at the Goeldi Museum with Dr. Rodolfo. Afternoon on the sidewalks outside the Grande Hotel, sipping on açaí. Night with Gastão Vieira and a poet. I read "Nocturne of Belo Horizonte," astounding the both of them. Gastão is unadulterated ease, delightful company.

FRESH

Frescal, when applied to pirarucu or duck in Marajó, means the meat is sun-dried, but just for a short time—twenty, thirty days at the most.

LOST

"I swear I don't remember coming through here!"

"Come on, now! . . . You girls can't even get your bearings in the brush, what sort of landowners are you, anyway? The ship's over there." I pointed that way, I was sure.

"No, sir! It's over there!" and Klein pointed at about a sixty-degree angle from me.

Then came a useless argument, each of us pointing in a different direction, and Musset the Frenchman was the only one not pointing anywhere. The girls were all worked up and I decided to act calmly. The fact was that we were good and lost, each of the five of us imagining that the others were keeping an eye on the path we'd taken. I burrowed deep into my sensory memory to see if I could remember what side of the ship the sun was on when we got off. At least that way, guided by the sun, we'd be able to make our way to the river, which was the first step in the solution. I didn't want to tell the others what I was thinking so they didn't confuse me with suggestions, but it seems the same thing had occurred to everyone, so that just as I was about to point in one direction saying it was that way, Scales pointed in the opposite direction, Trumpet pointed at a right angle to the left, and Klein pointed at a right angle to the right, and they exclaimed resolutely, *una voce*: "It's this way!"

Musset the Frenchman wasn't pointing anywhere. And for pity's sake, what a name at a time like this! . . .[110] I proposed that we settle down, and we took a seat to figure it out. Someone thought to go back to the shack on the lake to ask the crippled woman, but which way was the lake? And the argument kicked up again, what were we to do? That was when I laid out the situation as it really stood: two pretty girls, Musset the Frenchman, Klein the German, and a poet sitting around like dummies waiting for death surely couldn't be right. The sun was high by then, and it was quite hot out. A tiny hunger pang was born. Just then a handsome little river turtle came by, turned its head to look at us, and went on its way. We all immediately realized that this was a sign from above and decided to follow the turtle. After about an hour or so, we'd taken eight steps and could still see the roots where we'd sat down to figure things out. At this, a water snake slithered by at top speed, in exactly the opposite direction from the turtle, and we had the impression that this was also a sign from above, but these two signs were undeniably at odds. Then we realized that yes, they were signs from above, there was no doubt about that, but it so happened that the signs from above were too important to be worrying about our earthly salvation. Instead, they had come now, on the verge of our demise, to show us the two roads to postmortem salvation, the paths of Good and Evil. And we felt a chill in our bellies. That chill reminded us that we were starting to get hungry and we'd better eat something, some wild berry, or dig up a manioc root and roast it. This suggestion soon left us in dire straits of hunger and we decided to find the biggest manioc root we could find to truly fill our bellies. And we all set out looking for a manioc plant, but after about six minutes, except for Musset the Frenchman who wasn't looking for anything, I noticed that we were all walking hand in hand, whenever one took a step the others did too, all sneaking glances at one another instead of looking at the plants. It hit me: "Who here knows what a manioc plant looks like?"

Just as I'd suspected: they were city folk, fancy little land-owners, nobody there knew what a manioc plant looked like. But by then our hunger was so tremendous that when I spotted a colossal tree about three meters round, with fabulously huge roots, I imagined it might be the very manioc plant to sate our hunger. Everyone quickly agreed because we were all terribly wearied from arguing, and we got to it. Since we had no weap-ons, Musset the Frenchman and I started digging into the earth with our lickpots to grub up the biggest and tenderest manioc roots. Klein was off gathering dry leaves, nigh impossible to find round those soggy parts, to make a fire and fry up the manioc, since we've always been partial to fried manioc. Mean-while, the girls, armed with their hairpins and singing gentle melodies to lull our fatigued limbs, readied themselves to peel the manioc roots. Klein had managed to scrounge up about thirty dry leaves and a few more or less dry branches, but I re-membered in time that we only had a handful of matches, about twenty in all, and we ought to save them till the last. In a fit of fury I bawled the German out and stuck all the matches into my pocket. The German and the Frenchman, abruptly al-lied, exchanged a conniving glance and made as if to invade me, but Trumpet saw it all and saved the day. She snatched the matches out of my pocket and stuck them into her décolletage, declaring chastely, "Come get the matches if you dare!"

Then the foreigners retreated. But at this, Musset the French-man had a providential idea and cried out: "But then we won't be able to roast the manioc!"

"Oh, what hooey! The manioc's going to be fried, not roasted!"

Then Scales calmed me down, making me see that the Frenchman wasn't trying to fight anymore, and that any man-ioc, fried or roasted, needs a fire. I conceded that everyone was right that I was wrong and asked Trumpet for the matches, who handed them over reluctantly. After the twenty matches were gone, Klein the German remembered that with my glasses and a sunbeam it would be easier to make a fire, and this was our salvation. I lent Klein my glasses, and while he squinted up looking for a sunbeam, I started digging again. What a grind it was! but what truly made my gentlemanly soul ache was to see those two noble flowers of the São Paulo hothouse sitting there, serene and heroic, hairpins at the ready, just waiting for a manioc root to peel. I'd look over at them, rally myself, and plunge my lickpot into the dirt anew.

We dug and dug, and round about nightfall we'd gotten a good meter and a half of manioc root out of the ground. But how to cut through that mighty root? Hunger was darkening my vision, I couldn't resist, I took a bite out of the root, but it was so bitter that I gave a bitter smile. "This isn't manioc, my friends . . ."

They all came over straightaway to try the root and we came to the agreement that it was not in fact manioc. The German hadn't managed to make a fire with my glasses and was sitting there like a dummy, right in front of me, examining a pretty little butterfly he'd caught.

At this I flew into a rage and shoved him. "Beat it, you numb-skull!"

He jumped back when I pushed him, letting the butterfly go. But what lucky chance! Klein had jumped back onto a little gecko, and the poor thing was left there, unable to walk, its spine broken. We tried to fillet it as best we could with the hairpins, and after it was divvied up, we devoured that puny raw meal. The nourishment brightened up my view and I spied the dawn dripping from the branches. We all took heart at the day and came to the agreement that, before we set out in search of the riverbank, we'd best deal with our hunger once and for all. Then we started giving one another huge shoves to see if we might accidentally land on a few more geckos. Only then did I understand that admirable northern proverb: "Necessity is what makes a frog jump." And it was after one of those shoves that Musset the Frenchman landed on a swarm of ants and scampered off dancing one of Rameau's minuets. I went over to examine the ants, and in light of my previous experience, I made the triumphant diagnosis: "We have fire!"

It was the famous so-called fire ant. Having flayed the five geckos we'd accidentally hunted with our shoves, I deposited them on the swarm. The ants bit down on the meat, and it was soon properly smoked. We were about to sit down to our frugal repast when Klein the German, examining the legs of Musset the Frenchman, who was inconsolable over the bites, noticed that each bite had a little watery blister on it. He went straight over to fetch another fire ant, put it on the Frenchman's leg, and it bit down. Klein examined the bite and cried out. We rushed over in great distress, but Klein only smiled and said enigmatically: "All we have to do is follow this swarm, keeping the ants ahead of us, and we'll come to the river."

And he went on ahead. Well, we hadn't marched a quarter of an hour before we started hearing the Tapuios playing around as they carried logs onto the *Vitória*. And since they were all having so much fun, nobody had noticed we were gone. We shed tears of joy, saved from looming death, and commended Musset the Frenchman for having found the way out. The thing is, fire ants always fetch water from the river to keep their anthills from catching fire.

JULY 29

Going to Marajó. At five and plenty we take the *Ernestina* across the bay. Around eight, we get on the *Tucunaré*, a smaller boat, and go down the Arari River. Long stretches and little stops. Santana. Cachoeira. Paraíso with its buffaloes. São Joaquim, with its buffaloes. Only Brazilians would have thought to raise not only zebus but American buffaloes too; a cross between a sheep and a pig . . .[111] We're finally in another sort of Amazonian landscape. The Arari started out with a little scrubby forest along its banks and a few incomparably charming creekoids. The ingazeiras blanket the banks, leafy and plump, washing their branches in the river water. A few little

monkeys fly from branch to branch. The aningas in bloom.
Once in a while the hoatzins flying low, seeming to weigh a
ton. And an abundance of a purple creeper whose name nobody knows, covering the leafy banks. And the view opens up
onto new horizons. Immense fields, intense bright green, with
islands of forest off in the distance, standing out clearly, a dark
green that divides sky from field. Scales thinks of Scotland. I
agree eruditely, half-ruffled. This is Marajó, folks! Does Scotland have jacanas too? Herons?[112] Does it have this Arari
River, which never ends and tapers narrower and narrower,
leaving voluptuous impressions on your unbridled senses? . . .
Does Scotland have this hellscape of big-eared cattle, these
zebus and buffaloes, degrading the sublime beauty of these
fields! . . . Herons, herons, herons, a vividly pink spoonbill in
the air!

And finally we go by one perch that wrecks me with feeling.
There's no describing it, no imagining it. Thousands of scarlet
ibises, pink spoonbills, great white herons, jabirus, maguari
storks, white, black, gray, in the tall trees, on the bright green
grass. And when you make a noise on purpose, a shot in the
air, everything flies up in crazy flocks, not fleeing, flying, dancing in the air, reds, pinks, mottled whites, dappled in the bright
sun. I fell down onto the deck. People came to see, and it was
just that, I fell down! The emotion of it was so powerful that
my legs gave out, I fell down. To balance out the poetry of that
fall: I remember when I was a boy, rooting at football matches,
at one game between my beloved Paulistano and São Paulo
Athletic, when the latter scored the goal that stole the champi-
onship cup from me, I fell on the ground then.[113] But now I am
a man, hewn by experiences and pleasures. And the birdly
beauty of Marajó knocked me down to the ground. The others
laugh. Dona Olívia finds my tumble exceptionally funny. But I
believe her laughter is a bit forced. She'd like to fall down too,
in a fit of happiness like she's never known. Her pretty eyes are
exquisite today. Boatbills, maguaris, sunbitterns. Half scarlet
ibis, half moorhen. A varnished alligator makes a run for it and
flops into the water. A spoonbill in the middle of one, two,
three, thirteen jabirus. The cormorant, swimming with its

whole body in the water, just its slender neck and little head popping up, turns here, turns there, fleeing from us. But the boat is faster, and it takes off in dripping flight to hide itself far away. *Malhada* is the place where the cattle gather during the day, there's the malhada over there! Sportingly flat fields, drained of nature . . . An oriole blackbird, bright yellow and black, another with a scarlet back, black wings and head. A river turtle on a log, it drops into the water. And off in the distance, the smoke from the bush burning off . . .

Stopped at Tuiuiú, where we'll spend the night. It's unbearable. Billions, billions of mosquitoes. For the first time I can't resist, and I slather myself with that English ointment made from Java citronella—nice-smelling, by the way. I've got clumps of ointment on my face. But the mosquitoes come doggedly at my face, dig through the grease, bite, and die mired in the ointment. It's horrific. Dinner: eggs and dried duck. It stinks a bit when it's not well prepared, as was the case here. And we sing! We sing all the same, swallowing mosquitoes.

JULY 30

Noise and mosquitoes, I wake up at four-thirty. Hygiene courtesy of Florida Water, bought in Iquitos, which I hadn't seen or smelled since childhood. I become utterly nauseating. The noise gets louder, and round about six, with the sun up, they start loading cattle onto another boat bound for Belém. The cowhands, most of them mulattoes, bring me back to a more Afro-Brazilian normalcy after two months' time. Stocky, cheerful, turning work into play, as they do all across the North.

"Heeeey, buu! Heeey, buu!"

"C'meeeeeere, bull!"

"Grab 'im, brotha!"

"He going on the steamer or the launch?"

"Lower the line, brotha!"

"C'mere, bull! C'meeere, bull!"

"Dad-blame it! . . ."

"Heuuuu! . . ."

"Heaaaaaaa . . ."

And the bulls spill out of the little corral on the shore.

"Heeey, buu!"

"On the launch, pal!"

"C'mon, bull!"

The crane yells louder than all of them, hoisting the bull up by its horns. The bull rolls its wide-open eyes, neck doubled, stretched to the limit, lands on the launch, and straightens itself out. Doesn't budge, tho, still stunned with terror.

"Send that bull over!"

"Give us some bull, now!"

"Thissun's for the launch, brotha!"

While the farm operator, "my apologies," offers us some watery, "low-water" milk.

We set off. It's past ten by the time we make our way into the mouth of Lake Arari at the center of the island. To our left, inert and doubled in the still waters of the lake, is the lacustrine settlement of Jenipapo. Today is horrifyingly "exceptional." We go out in a rowboat around the lake. I take an oar, clumsy as all get-out. The heat beats down. They say it'll be bad if it catches us out on the lake at full strength. From the launch, they call us back. We set off, taking a shortcut along the village's watery roads, and just after eleven the *Tucunaré* heads off to the river and back to Belém, running from the heat. We all sway, a wash of seasickness, it's eleven-fifty on the dot and the *Tucunaré* has run aground! And thus begins, the crew begins, the work of freeing it. They empty the boilers to see if it'll float, nothing doing. And so it goes. The heat beats down and down. The sky is white, reflecting off utterly white waters, a ferocious whiteness, nerve-racking, blinding, absurd, prying into your eyes, nostrils, pores, there's no resisting it, I feel I'm about to die, Lord have mercy! Best stay still, don't even talk. We begin to live another life, a metallic life, harsh, with no entrails. I do not exist. And then I catch the hope of a breeze on the air, yes, it is a breeze. The white sky darks up in heavy cloud grays. In five minutes the sky is completely dark ash and a strong agreeable breeze blows, born from the deep waters. It doesn't manage to rain, but the heat has gone, it's four o'clock by now. Given the uselessness of the efforts so far, they dispatch a canoe downriver in search of help.

But we're already better at living this equatorial life. There's no question that it's more objective than our life down south. It's not exactly a matter of more or less spirituality on our part, but rather the spirituality of things. I don't know, a landscape on the outskirts of São Paulo, a little town, a river in Minas, a farm in São Paulo, an orange tree, a peroba rosa tree, I don't know . . . I feel, when I contemplate them, that there's something to them that I don't understand, some inner life that's shielded from me, a mysterious soul to things. That's it: the soul of things. From the dunes of the Northeast on, the soul of things has vanished. Everything is sheathed in a violent, perfectly outlined epidermis that has no mystery to it. Frankness, a certain honest brutality, things just being things. And the result is a sensuality of contact in which we're all infected with violent sensorial life, it's inebriating.

I can't properly eat dinner with this irony hanging over me. The first to spot them called everyone over. And we lingered a long time, watching the piranhas in the water, ravenous lightning bolts in gray and scarlet, eating meat. They eat meat, and how! Now I have the impression that all the piranhas are spying on us from down in the water, marveling and remarking to one another that we eat meat . . .

And night comes. Trumpet sings and plays guitar. The blessing, the delight that is lying down out on the roof in the strong breeze that whisks the mosquitoes away . . . The delight that is stretching out on the roof under a wrong-headed sky where the clouds are the night and the firmament behind is bright, bright, a luminous faded green . . . The blessing that is letting yourself live with nothing more, no tomorrow, no yesterday, heedlessly flooding your tongue with the last cold guaranás . . . The blessing that is a night with a strong breeze, whisking all your thoughts away, at the mouth of Lake Arari . . .

Jenipapo—at the mouth of Lake Arari

JULY 31

Day breaks and all of a sudden the *Tucunaré* gets free on its own, effortlessly. We set off. Around eight o'clock we meet the *Flecha*, sent to aid us. It's slimmer, executes an elegant about-face and goes on ahead of us with a heron's grace, its wake woven with solar hues pointing the way for the bumbling old *Tucunaré*. We leave the "pilot" at Tuiuiú. It's still late morning when we go by Arari Farm. Afternoon outing in Santana. Wading, wary of stingrays. At nightfall we set off again on the *Ernestina*, in search of Belém. At eight fifty-five on the dot we run aground right in the middle of Guajará Bay, with Belém before us. A mild grounding, this: fifteen minutes later, the launch has "rhode it through," as they'd say on the *Vitória*. An hour later, Belém. Have to see to my bags, since tomorrow, what with goodbyes and the rest, there'll be no time.

AUGUST 1

Last day in Belém, and I swear it's a soul-stirring thing. Never in my life had I been so pleased with a city, taken such a liking to it. On the score of bliss-gorging, I spent the best days of my life in Belém, unforgettable days. Morning of shopping, tickets, botherations, otter pelts, the market, Belém's greatest triumph, as always . . . Indian things . . . I buy a few in the end, it's all a bit silly. The prevailing Brazilian lack of organization is such that everything that the Indians sell at the Belém market is legitimate. It's all quite ugly, worthless, used. It has yet to occur to anyone that falsification is the way to make these things worth more, not just making them prettier and more valuable than the Indians do, but also making the Indians' things more valuable precisely by making them legitimate and rarer. The false document is what makes the true one legitimate. And value never really lies in truth per se, but in legitimacy, don't you think? I don't really know if I do, but since I've already written it, might as well let it stand. Chalk it up to the prevailing disorganization. Lunch. I run off and visit the two magnificent baroque churches, just magnificent. Visit to the governor. Farewells. And . . . and, as always happens when the moment comes and everything is ready for a trip, it's still afternoon, just barely afternoon now, the *Baependi* will set off at eight o'clock, and . . . and nothing! A gaping hole in life. We have nothing to do.

But there's this sidewalk outside the Grande Hotel, the plaza and its enormous leafy trees, and iced açaí, can it be that I really like açaí? Like isn't quite the word, but in Belém, açaí certainly can be fun. It's one of those "local" foods that, even if they're not tasty, are such a part of the place that it puts up a wall if you don't partake. And it's impolite not to like it. Açaí isn't exactly bad . . . It lands softly in your mouth, there's a sweet taste of trampled weeds, not the taste of any fruit or leaf. And soon it becomes a warm ease in your mouth, a hint of nostalgia, a far-off twinge of bitterness that's not quite bitter, pleasant in its own way. A thick drink that, no matter how much ice is added to it, always has a friendly, humble, obliging degree of warmth. Açaí has a peculiar charm . . . You start liking it to be nice and then keep on liking it because you feel bad for it. And here I speak for us, folks who don't need to live on açaí, the milk of the poor, folks who drink it to kill time on our out-and-aboutings. Açaí isn't exactly bad, far from it, but it's a long way from being good, as good as duck with tucupi sauce, crab in the shell, and fourteen other Amazonian tidbits. And there's a psychology to it. I feel profoundly local, well and truly localized, when I'm having iced açaí. Finally dinner.

It's time to go, and we've got two anecdotes. One: in the morning, I gave the reporter the interview he'd requested to telegraph to Rio de Janeiro. I'm having dinner and I see the fellow, twentyish, standing at the door of the dining room and looking at me. When I head to my room—I'd decided to change my clothes, they're distinctly wrinkled at the end of the day and the whole of officialdom will be there at the dock—the fellow stops me midway, hemming and hawing. What is it? I ask a bit impatiently. He, quite fretful, stuttering: "You know that part of your interview, sir . . . ?"

"Yes, what about it?"

"Well, to break things up a bit, I added that you smiled and took a drag on your cigarette, that's all right, isn't it?"

His eyes were filled with distress, begging for approval.

"That's just fine, pal!"

I've gained an admirer. Perhaps a friend . . .

The second anecdote might well be called "The Price of Amazonia." I'm setting off with just fourteen mil-réis in my pocket, my money's simply evaporated. Besides my own expenses, I've been lending money to the girls, who at this point are embarrassed to ask Dona Olívia for more, and this is the result, tips given, all paid up, I've got fourteen mil-réis to my name. I was hastily changing my clothes, already down to my shorts, when a knock came at the door. It was a package.

"Reply requested."

Thoroughly bedeviled, I open up the package: it's a little book on Amazonia, full of profiles of politicians. An accompanying card described the author's sentiments, as follows:

Dr. Mário de Andrade. Sir: Trusting in your keen observational spirit and fine perspicacity as regards the grand future that awaits Amazonia, we humbly submit this work for your consideration in the hopes that this copy may be accepted for the sum you should deem that the subject deserves, which may be delivered to the bearer. From your humble servant, So-and-So Fleabite Small Potatoes [sic].

What now? How much is Amazonia worth? Especially for such an enthusiastic, grateful sojourner as myself . . . Twenty milréis, I said to myself. Then I was in a fix. I didn't have twenty mil-réis on me, and the book was going to be a pain, my bags were already packed and stuffed full of Amazonia. I had two fives and the rest in coins. I opened the door a crack (on account of my undergarments) and stuck five mil-réis out:

"Will that do?"

The money was snatched from my hand, not so much as a thanks. The governor's aide takes us to the boat in an official car. Mayor Crespo de Castro, Bebê Costa, Dr. Caper, Miss MacDowell, Gastão Vieira, who gives me a Panama hat as a present. And our servant Raimundo, providential Raimundo, who accompanied us the whole journey through, providing refreshments with uncanny timing. He's got tears in his eyes as he waves to us, our Raimundo. The *Baependi* lumbers away from the dock amidst these disagreeable departure protocols. I say goodbyes and more goodbyes. Clóvis Barbosa too. I've grown quite friendly with Gastão Vieira. Nice folks. Nice folks, off in the distance. Farther off. The steamer picks up speed from a soft sea breeze. The night is dark, deep. Belém shines in the distance.

We were all atremble . . . etc.

"Mário . . ."

I jumped.

"What is it, Queen?"

"With all the goodbyes, I wasn't able to get money out of the bank. Would you mind lending me some for the trip?"

This lands like a punch to the stomach: I'm left reeling. Once she's caught up, she just smiles, the consummate traveler. She has about twenty or thirty mil-réis. We'll take on debts, which we can pay in Rio de Janeiro. But I can't swallow this humiliation. I go to bed all out of sorts.

THE POEM IS BORN

Precisely on the 23rd of November, in this year 1927, *Clã do jabuti* was about to go to press, and as I was looking over the proofs I had a shock. In the title "Song of the Porto Alegre Jail," there it was, overlooked: "Song of the Alegre Porto Jail!" Even before I could make the correction, the answer was born within me: the *alegre porto*, the joyful port, isn't Porto Alegre, it's Belém . . . And I walked out of the press taken with the idea, Belém is the "joyful port" . . . and in reliving fresh memories, strolling absent-mindedly, smiling, happy, walking along, rhythms were born in me, whole verses . . . As soon as I'd gotten home, almost without the slightest correction, with the stanzas in the right order and the refrain in the right place, I gave birth to this song:

SONG OF THE JOYFUL PORT

Ruby-red fishermen's sails all ablaze
Colorful sails to catch the sun's rays
Muddy brown waters of rivers and seas
Mango trees, mango trees, palm trees and palm trees
And my little Barbadian, wherever you are!

What a joyful port,
Belém do Pará!

What a port of joy, Belém do Pará!
Let's go to the market, there'll be mungunzá!
Let's go to the bay, there'll be boats in the breeze!
Let's go out on the streets, there'll be mango trees!
Let's go out on the terrace to drink guaraná!

Oh, joyful port,
Belém do Pará!

The sluggish sun on the gentle shore,
Heat beating down with the force of an oar,
How good it is to sleep through the day!
What light! what joy! what melancholy!
And my little Barbadian, wherever you are!

What a joyful port,
Belém do Pará!

The little Barbadian, wherever she is
Grazing the white of the fellows in linen
Strolling in Souza, what a lovely expedition!
In the shadow of a vast leafy mango tree,
Just after the just-'bout-to-rain, then, ah! . . .

Oh, little Barbadian,
Belém do Pará!

There's fun to be had, more than New York or Vienna!
Just one violet glance from one morena
The mixed-drink sort, a Brazilian cocktail,
Fills you up better than an açaí palm,
That sweet taste when man meets woman!
Pause in Pará and you'll want for nothing more!
Try the tucupi! Try the tacacá!

What a joyful port,
Belém do Pará!

AUGUST 2

Salt water bearing us south . . . I wake up at five and take an
hour to wash up in clear water. I'd had baths like these in

Belém, I mustn't be unfair, but there was always a lingering, ir-repressible hint of the muddy waters of the river and the baths on board. I feel good as new. I take the choppiness in stride with no seasickness whatsoever. The *Baependi* is a cargo ship. We eat in Dona Olívia's cabin. Then I talk about all sorts of things with Cholito. Who's Cholito? Not worth going into. He came with us from Iquitos on the *São Salvador*. The tempera-ture goes down as the wind blows and the clouds cast a shadow. After my afternoon ablutions, I don my southern clothes, cash-mere after two months of absence. And I'll be damned if I didn't get all adagio! I feel an urge to be alone, to be sad . . . I flee from the saloon, the girls, I'm going to be alone, I'm going to be sad, out on the bow with nobody around, in this ugly night. I get vaguely dejected. I feel completely alone. My body sings, vibrating in the wind.

AUGUST 3

Dawn finds us peeking at Graça Aranha's homeland. São Luís up ahead, there's no getting off, just a quick stop, a dense clus-ter of rooftops and green treetops. No sign of life. The sun is burning down. São Luís is one with the Brazilian Whole,[114] thoroughly stupefied. At ten we set off. I go off to do some gymnastics to fix my body, which has been pretty well de-formed by two months on board and cold drinks on the hour. The caica parrot swallows a pearl off Dona Olívia's necklace and takes on the miffed air of a Cleopatra. Sea blue here, light green there, with dark patches. I get a telegram from my friend in Natal, Luís da Câmara Cascudo, who I've never seen in my life and who I like so well. "Prefer reception with or without speech?" I reply: "Without." Splendid winds.

AUGUST 3, SATIRE (GRAÇA ARANHA)

I'm getting a taste for ditties. I hit upon another, today's better than yesterday's. It must've been the trip to our international

lands—downtown, São Paulo, Rio, work, artistic struggles—
that got me thinking of Graça Aranha. And this little poem
came out:

> A writer once fancied himself
> A guide to Guarani verse
> But we've told him a thousand times
> As an escort he couldn't be worse

Particularly in Rio, there are all sorts of Brazilian modernists
who are erudite in modernism. But you can very well be erudite
in a thing without ever actually knowing a thing about it . . .

AUGUST 4

Life on board, fantastic gusts. Wind and more wind. Dona
Olívia doesn't get up. I am left admirably alone, shredded by
the winds. More gymnastics. The ship bucks. Two salty baths
a day. Starboard, the alabaster monotony of the dunes.
Nothing.

AUGUST 5

Across from Fortaleza. We get off at ten. Automobile from here
to there, through an air of cleanliness. Market, where I buy a
carnaúba mat and some delicious guava jam. Uninteresting
churches and the lovely Parque da Liberdade. Lunch at the Ro-
tisserie, vatapá with coconut milk, wonderful! I conscientiously
take note of all my bills, paid with money from god knows
who, the barman? the captain? passed along by Dona Olívia. I
always divvy up common expenses, with the peevish honesty
of the poorest at the table—which is not without its serious in-
conveniences for me. Dona Olívia takes me to task, gets ruf-
fled, and I take myself to task too! I know it's foolish, but when
it comes time to pay up, I can't help myself! What an idiot I am.
The road to Maranguape, coconut milk at the Balneário,

Iracema Beach. I'm perverse enough to commit the unthinkable act of hunting for little shells on Iracema Beach—I feel as vile as virginity. Baturité railroad?

"Uh-huh."

"Thank you."

"Don't mention it."

Hard time setting off, rough seas. Manaus had the Church of the Poor Devil, and Fortaleza has the Church of the Great Little One . . .

AUGUST 6

In Areia Branca, port of Mossoró. Four cargo steamers, barges . . . Thirty-two jangadas soaring bright white, settling into the rough waters bit by bit. We don't get off, we're far out from the beach. The sailing barges are putting up a hard fight in these rough waters, pulling alongside the *Baependi* with astonishing skill, loaded up with cotton, salt, and china clay.

"Artus, your bag's already off, ain't it?"

"Throw it down, Chico!"

"Wasn't it you brought a bag?"

"Sure was."

"Gimme a hand to pass it over, will you?"

"Uh-huh."

"Quit that bag-dragging, now!"

"Drop them bags!"

And then, from out of a gaggle of decrepit old ladies, they hoisted up a child of about four or five, with an expression of such inconceivable terror that nobody could bear to meet it—we all turned our faces away.

It's almost seven o'clock, a tempestuous dusk, and we're setting off.

"Hey, Chico Chagas!"

"What?"

"There's three packages of yours here!"

"No there ain't! Is there?"

The other fellow busts out laughing and spreads the wings of his sailing barge. Chico Chagas busts out laughing too. He's black, good-looking, with all his teeth. And his barge is named *Liberty*. Its name is *Liberty*.

AUGUST 7

Beautiful approach to Natal, around noon. The Potengi River is gentle. Fort of the Magi on the port side. We're finally in Rio Grande do Norte, the personal property of my friend Luís da Câmara Cascudo, now which one is he? Dozens of little boats are pulling up to the *Baependi*. And then I spot a young fellow waving hugely, just like the style of Cascudinho's letters, that had to be him. And it really was. On land, introductions, O'Grady the pleasant mayor, the general secretary. Cars. Marvelous Areia Preta Beach, Petrópolis, Refoles, Reservatório. I visit the poet Jorge Fernandes, holed up in his house. Beer at the little restaurant. And dinner at the Escola Doméstica, which is Natal's Butantan. No speech. We set off well into the night. Life on board, getting ready for bed.

AUGUST 8

Around seven o'clock, Cabedelo, in the thick of an invasion of beggars. No time to go to the city of Paraíba.[115] Nobody wants to get off. I get off and stroll around on my own, accompanied only by a pilot from the *Baependi*. Photos, a little doll-sized hammock, coconut water, green coconuts, magnificent bananas, little toy rafts. We set off two hours later. Life on board. Since Fortaleza we've been voyaging in the company of the curious social phenomenon, all too familiar to travelers, which goes by the name of the Brazilian Family. Oh, but who has never encountered that strange navigational phenomenon, the Brazilian Family! It looks like this: a handsome enough but seemingly exhausted man, making listless gestures that inevitably wind up in him scratching his half-kinky hair. He heeds the calls of a washed-out, gaunt Indian wife, dressed in the second-to-latest fashion with great self-assurance. Only her hair is somewhat indecisive, attempting to creep across her face, which features a pair of pretty staring eyes and an absolutely desolate "For heaven's sake! These children!" Then she squats down right there to break up the fight between the two littlest ones, both of which are howling because Zezé stole Arlindinha's candy and is now sucking on it till kingdom come, spattering the deck with his alabaster drool. Mrs. Washed-Out sticks her never-endingly long index finger into Zezé's howling mouth, it looks like she's killing him, wiggles the finger around in there and finally locates the candy, removes the selfsame and drops it into Arlindinha's hands. Arlindinha then, out of pure spite, hurls the candy, which is a gumdrop, onto the spotless deck. The despairing wife calls her husband over again and asks for his handkerchief as she listlessly gestures at the gumdrop stuck to the deck. He lends her his handkerchief, and she just barely wipes down Zezé's sugar-sticky hand. Then the husband, who stands a bit more on ceremony, looks this way and that, but what's a man to do, we're right there, he bends down, grabs the gumdrop, and tosses it into the sea. But Arlindinha had only thrown it away out of spite, and so when she sees her father toss the candy overboard, she lets loose such piercing shrieks that even more folks gather around. The mother, who's sitting in my chair, rented out by me, rocking Zezé on her lap, says with the utmost calm: "That's all right, now, Arlindinha, Mama'll buy you some more gumdrops later."

But Arlindinha won't stop crying, and father and mother rock away in that familiar wailing, sitting on our chairs on the portside deck, which is the side with the fresh sea breeze. If anyone is bothered by the children's wretched sobbing, the mother and father smile, saying that that's just how it is. And for the forty-seventh time the wife says limply, "Hush, now, Zezé," and the husband says awkwardly, "Don't cry, now, Arlindinha" . . . and that's all. And the two of them, children on their laps, drift off for a nap in your very own chairs, but only after the wife has given your very own clothes a good hard look and directed a scolding look at her husband. It's clear what she's saying inside: "You see! That's the kind I wanted to buy, the one you thought wasn't decent!" The kids' wailing is dying down, and we might as well just wait here. There's no use going to the starboard deck, which is the province of the three eldest scions of the Brazilian Family, three burly little males in their short pants, already smoking, playing at throwing a hard rubber ball that never hits them, they're so clever that they duck: it only ever hits other people. In the saloon, the eldest heiress, with a languid air, pouts if you should enter and interrupt her flirting with the steward.

Around two in the afternoon, we're able to find some distraction in Recife, under a splendid sun. I'd telegraphed ahead to Ascenso Ferreira, asking for money. No Ascenso on the dock. So we went to see the manatee.

THE MANATEE

Going to see the manatee was certainly the best part. It eats grass quite politely, making no noise whatsoever, only half opening its mouth. If it could talk, I'd teach it Italian and have it sit in a restaurant in São Paulo to teach my compatriots how to dine. Unfortunately, it can't talk. The manatee is a whale that only stopped growing because it didn't feel like it anymore. It has a face like a hippopotamus and always keeps its eyes modestly below the waterline. Its fins are of a sort of silvery metal, from the platinum family, and may be used to make a grease that cures diseases of the liver, congestions, mosquito bites, and lumbago. For bruises, there's nothing better. The manatee lays pink eggs that are incubated in the sun by the city government. The little ones come out with tiny wings (these they soon shed), which they use to reach the waters of the Amazon and swim to Lake Lauricocha, where they grow to the age of reason. We appreciated the manatee very much indeed.

Dinner at Leite. A gloomy air is misting down over the night. My companions head back on board while I go look for

Inojosa. He's not in Recife, they tell me at the newspaper. I
head back on board, no Ascenso. A fine, cold drizzle. I go out
looking for Ascenso. Suddenly I'm at the river. I head back in
the opposite direction and suddenly I'm at the river again. Out-
and-out rain now. Downtown is deserted. No idea which way
I should go. It occurs to me to hail a car, but I haven't got any
money. I can't even quite remember Ascenso's new address. I'm
completely soaked. I feel cold. A few stragglers come down the
street, which is utterly deserted. I think they've come to arrest
me. No, they've come to rob me. I laugh out loud. The men
look at me, a little startled.

"Could you please tell me which way the docks are?"

They very graciously point the way.

"Thank you very much."

"Don't mention it."

I get back on board in tatters, at midnight.

AUGUST 9

Life on board. The Brazilian Family also harbors a so-called
blond exception, a descendant of the Dutch, to hear the Per-
nambucans tell it. I didn't name her yesterday because she was
poorly, her mother tells us, some bowel complaint. Her name is
Gracette, swear to God, and she must be about six, older than
Zezé and Arlindinha but younger than the three stocky boys.
Her father comes over and says: "Gracette, who's the prettiest
girl on the boat?"

"Meeeee."

"Well, see now, Gracette, that gentleman's saying you're ugly."

Gracette is dismayed, her lips quiver, she grabs onto her father's hand: "Go on and lie that I'm ugly, see if I care!"

And she bursts into tears. Then the father lends the mother
his handkerchief etc. Maceió ahoy, three o'clock in the afternoon. We get off on a sailboat. Car ride. We go to Bebedouro,
up on the heights, to contemplate the lakes: this is the Butantan
of Maceió. No—the Butantan of Maceió is the charru mussel,
a bowlful savored on board, the sublimest thing in the world.

What tender gentleness, the sweet taste of the firm, hearty flesh. Maceió, a homely little place . . .

AUGUST 10

Life on board, waiting for the *Bahia*, which only shows up in the afternoon. I'm the first to spot Tarsila and Osvaldo on the dock, catching us by surprise. Joy beyond boundless. Outings roaring with laughter. Dinner at the Petisqueira Baiana, the heaviest dinner in the world: vatapá, moqueca, and efó. Efó is the only masochistic dish I know of. As you eat it, you have the convulsive feeling of being eaten from the inside. It's terrible but delicious. On board. Who'd even think of sleeping! Paulista chitchat, witticisms, art. Osvaldo shows up in a wildly garish suit jacket, yellow, brown, and black, in utter sartorial sincerity.

AUGUST 11

There was no August 11 in 1927.

AUGUST 12

Shortly after lunch we made a sensational entrance into Vitória, Guanabara Bay ad usum delphini.[116] It's marvelous! We put our hands on everything. But after all that Northeast, when we get off on the dock, we start seeing folks *grandeur nature*. Market. I buy a clay zebu. Osvaldo's fixations: we got into two trotting automobiles and went up to the little town of Serra, indignant at the ease with which we made our way up the mountain. And after wasting all that time, we weren't able to visit the Great Tibetan Lama who lives in the Penha Convent up on Mount Athos. Dinner at José Portuga. Awful. Moonlit visit to Comprida Beach. There's always moonlight and there's always a beach—lovely. We got back on board around midnight.

AUGUST 13

At six-fifteen precisely we set off from Vitória, surrounded by
sensational colors. Life on board unpleasant, getting through
this last maritime leg of the journey—it's no journey anymore
and we're still-not-there, a stupid feeling. Around eleven P.M.,
the Cabo Frio lighthouse in view. I'd better pack my bags and
see if I can manage to get some sleep. A storm comes down and
goes on through morning, delaying the ship.

AUGUST 14

And here we are at long last in the vast Guanabara Bay, where
the sun resides. It's drizzling. We get off at nine. Jaime Ovalle,
Dante Milano, Manu, Antônio Bento, I'm ravingly happy. But
I run to the Copacabana Palace to borrow money from Paulo
Prado and pay off my debts. And I don't rest until I've paid ev-
erything, down to my tickets on the night train to São Paulo.
Lunch at the Minhota with Osvaldo, Tarsila, Dolur.[117] Then
whiskey with coconut water (really not the same thing, here) at
Casa Simpatia, Antônio Bento, Mary, Manu, the group. Din-
ner at a greasy spoon. At the station, Prudentinho and Iná, Sér-
gio Buarque de Holanda, Gallet, Luísa, Mary, Manu, Ovalle,
Dante Milano, Dodô. We set off: Dona Olívia, Goffredo da
Silva Telles, Clóvis Camargo, and I.

AUGUST 15

São Paulo, the bitter delight of unhappy souls . . . Train derails
in front of us, stopping us in Luís Carlos just before Moji. Dona
Olívia and company set off in a car that arrives for them. I turn
down a seat, waiting for my own people. Stupid decision, distress. I have a car brought from Moji for me, and in this state
of pure vexation I'm forced to share it with a stranger to boot,
one Mr. Abelardo César, who offers to go along with me and
split the cost. I say yes to the company, what am I to do! and

refuse the split, the car was already paid for and I'd find myself indelicate if I accepted. Worst of all, I miss meeting up with my family and friends, who'd taken a car and gone out to fetch me. For pity's sake! Finally, round two o'clock, it's precisely two-eleven and twelve seconds, I'm in "my" house, with "my" folks. Make sure the door's good and shut, Bastiana![118] Shut it and lock it up, Bastiana! and toss the key out the window!

APPENDIX

THE PAROARA IN THIRD CLASS AND OTHER STORIES

These little fables appear to have been written at some point after the trip; in Andrade's papers, they are typed or written out on separate slips from the rest of the travelogue.

OF HOW I MET THE AMAZONS
(SATIRE OF THE MODERN WOMAN)

I only find them along the Madeira River, from which they derived their name, calling themselves the Sticksinthemud.

They loved to say swear words, this being an ostentatious way of showing off their freedom and independence.

They were in a transitional phase, abandoning the old laws. But they had no new laws yet, so the whole thing was a three-ring circus.

They liked to show off their erudition. Sporting as all get-out, and strong too. They didn't stop at burning off one breast—now they had none at all, just like Antinous.

Philosophy, sociology, psychoanalysis. They were complexed as could be and didn't believe in God.

From the olden times, they had preserved only the art of the tear—not because this feminine practice came naturally to them, but so as to better bend merchants to their will.

They gave their children away to grandmothers and nannies but liked to raise animals and had a particular fondness for incandescent vampire fish.

They hated novels, but some were poets and others wrote short stories.

The Sticksinthemud are generally quite afraid of cockroaches, this being the reason why many emigrate, heading naturally to São Paulo.

THE SAINT IN THE ROCK[119]

A Paroara in third class tells me this story: the Saint in the Rock, near the town of Bonito, out in the country in Pernambuco, nobody'd seen her, folks prayed to her, would go out there, give her a calf, a chicken, money, still nobody'd ever seen her, just a vanishing few. One day a young fellow went out there and adored the saint for days on end. Pilgrimages and whatever the hell else were in full swing, and the Government, fearing another Juazeiro incident,[120] went and sent some troops out there to put a stop to it. The sergeant ordered the saint to come out from the rock, she didn't, he ordered her to, nothing doing. At long last, she came out. It was a young woman and she was pregnant. Just a little while ago, a granddaughter of hers died in the city of Recife.

JOSÉ ALBANO

I'm remembering what Paulo Prado and his son told me about José Albano. Now, José Albano was from Ceará.[121]

He spoke all sorts of living languages, all the main ones and Arabic, and had a good grasp of Latin and classical Greek.

He was tall, pale, bearded, tremendously handsome. Always had a great big knife in his waistcoat and could throw it like nobody's business.

They said that in Spain he'd given a talk and the critics swore that nobody after Cervantes had ever written such graceful and perfect Spanish.

He'd say in his madness that he couldn't live in France because the Académie Française, seeing that he wrote better than any of them and was a more accomplished master of the secrets of the pen, had set Clemenceau against him, the result being his expulsion from the latter's life and from France.

One day he went to visit Paulo Prado in a hotel in London.

Paulo Caio: "My father's in the bath."

José Albano: "How Greek of him!"

He walked into Paulo Caio's office in London, serenely removed his cape (he was always shrouded in a large cape), and with a swift motion made the knife leap out and rest quivering in the wood of the desk. He caressed its handle and said: "I am going to France to kill Clemenceau. My only protectors, Paulo Caio, are you and the consul. But now Clemenceau, who loathes me for knowing all his secrets, has set me against George V, and this I can bear no longer."

He put the knife away, wrapped himself in the cape, sat down in a corner of the office, and stayed there a while. Then he left quietly.

The consul arranged for four of his sonnets to be published in the *Times*. And there in the *Times* supplement a critic said that if all of Shakespeare's sonnets were not known to us, those four would undoubtedly have been attributed to him.

He'd say: you think the Inquisition is over in Brazil? Well, it's not. It still exists in a convent in Recife, hidden away from the world. (Here a succinct description of the convent, the landscape, the medieval Brazilian life led by the friars, and description of the torture he suffered.) But do you know how I held out? That was when I learned the art of ubiquity (is the word really *ubiquity*?). When they came to torture me the second time, I left my body and let it suffer—what horrors I made out on my poor face, with what melancholy I contemplated my tortured limbs, my grimaces! Once the torture was over, I entered my body again.

That was also why I didn't die when I dueled with the Baron

of Rio Branco. The bullet went in through my sacrum, put eighteen holes in my intestines, and having pierced my heart, deflected by the bulk of my lung, penetrated my spine and, taking an ascendant trajectory, came to rest in my brain matter, in the (such and such) lobe. I toppled over on my face while my adversary, nervously wiping the beads from his brow, murmured, "What a great Latinist he was." But I had departed my body and was wandering through the dawn of the caves. I returned to it later, once everything had calmed down.

But what people said was that the Baron of Rio Branco, observing José Albano's prodigious intelligence, set him to work far too hard. Hence the young man's madness.

Even the Inquisition in Recife could be explained. The poet had been sent to a madhouse there, and he certainly took a beating, as part of the many treatments for derangement of which nurses and men in general are capable.

THE FATHER OF THE CEARENSES[122]

Today, the Paroara in third told me quite the spicy story—I'm not sure if I should even repeat it . . .

Word has it, in the olden days, the Cearenses were physically more gifted than any man on earth. Nobody could ever bet against them when it came to the preambles and the enlengthenings of the pleasure of love, for not only were the Cearenses powerfully endowed, but of what each mortal man had only a pair, they had no fewer than four. With them, that old empress wouldn't just tire out, she'd be more than satisfied. But it all happened when they went to the Amazon. You see, the Father of all Cearenses was quite the looker, the kind of man described above, but really exceptionally well equipped and well disposed. So well disposed that he refused to surrender to suffering when the first real droughts came to the Northeast. "Let's go to the Amazon," he said. "There's water there." And he set off with all the Paroaras.

Well then: he got here, and he really was a powerful man, he made himself a pile of money, and whenever it got too big, he'd sidle over to Manaus to spend it. He'd light his cigar with a five hundred mil-réis bill, he'd lose eighty thousand in a night at the table without batting an eye. Soon he became the greatest gambler in the Amazon, to match his reputation as the greatest lover in the world. That's right, a married man for him meant less than nothing, and the married ladies were satisfied as could be.

Well, wouldn't you know it, the Father of all Cearenses up and stopped flirting with them all! It was a fearful scandal, all anybody could talk about, until they found out why. The Father of all Cearenses was now nothing less than husbanded up with the Iara herself. See, one day his reputation made its way all the way to the vast river's bed, and the Iara got jealous as could be. Sitting atop that heap of skeletons that had all let her down, she conjured up a picture of the Cearense who was so rich that he had not two, but four nuquiiris. Then she had a marriage proposal sent to him, 'cause with goddesses it's marriage or bust, no special-friendliness or bigamy. Give me dependence or give me death.

So the hero accepted the glory of being the Iara's husband, only a Cearense could ever be worthy of it. The goddess imposed one condition, which he swore to without a second thought, even chuckling to himself: whenever desire struck and she called, he'd have to drop his work, drop everything and go down to the river bottom to play around. And son, it was sublime. On their wedding night plenty of fish died, so overcome with awe at the struggle between those two powerful lovers that they forgot to breathe. The goddess's thirst was never quenched, but who ever saw the Father of all Cearenses falter! Then dawn broke and the Father of all Cearenses had to go out to the rubber plantation, and so he did. That terrific energy . . . In an hour's time, he hacked away at seventy rubber trees, but now and again he'd stop what he was doing and chuckle to himself. The Father of all Cearenses was recalling the nice night he'd had.

Well, hadn't been two hours when a little bee came buzzing by, buzzed right around his head and told him that the Iara was in the mood again and wanted him back. He nodded and went.

He came back half an hour later, a little red in the face, and every so often the bee would come buzzing over 'cause the Iara was calling. And there the Father of all Cearenses went.

Now it so happened that by the end of that harvest, he'd heaped up over two hundred thousand, making him the richest man in the world. So he was fixing to put that bundle of money on the gambling table in Manaus. He talked to the goddess and she said right away that arrangements could be made, she'd move to her palace on the bottom of the Rio Negro, and so they went.

When the Father of all Cearenses got to Manaus round about noon, he went straight to the casino. It was early, and how, but he could always put up a mean game of baccarat. But hadn't been two hours, and he'd lost just twenty thousand, when the bee came buzzing over and told him—well, you know. The Father of all Cearenses excused himself quite politely, saying he was just going to the little boys' room. When he turned his back everyone laughed, since just about everyone knew what a lucky man he was.

Half an hour later the Father of all Cearenses came back, a little red in the face, and they got back to the game. After another two hours the bee came over, buzzing away, buzz-buzz-buzz, and the Father of the Cearenses had lost a good thirty-five thousand. He excused himself, went off, and the game had already been interrupted four times when the bee came over with that hellish little buzz, buzz-buzz-buzz, and now the Father of all Cearenses was up by fifteen clams. Now this was too much, and our hero shouted out, mad as could be, "I ain't leavin' this game! Tell her to go plant potatoes!" The bee went off.

It was already past midnight, everyone was bone tired, and the Father of all Cearenses had lost all his riches. When had he ever gotten back to his riverbed home after nightfall! The goddess would be furious . . . But no, she wasn't. When he got there he shaved his whiskers so he wouldn't prickle her up and made his way over to that lovely bed of silver and gold, a little wary, but why doubt! the Iara even smiled at him, all languid, and raised those beautiful arms, the color of fresh milk from a rubber tree. And the Father of all Cearenses, moved by the depths of her love, dived down into that bliss.

And what bliss! one he'd never felt before, so new! It was strange . . . the pleasure had never opened up so far and then closed up again, closing and closing like a magnet that bound everything to it, down to his nuquiiris! The Father of all Cearenses hollered out, delighted and surprised: "What in tarnation are you gettin' up to, lady?" he exclaimed.

"I'm planting potatoes."

He didn't rightly understand and went to hide his head in the Iara's beautiful green locks, but then he put two and two together and horror struck. He tried to pull away from the goddess but realized he was stuck. Then the Father of all Cearenses, who really was a powerful man, bellowed like a bull and wrenched so hard that it sent a tidal wave down all the rivers. But the Father of all Cearenses managed to free himself, bloody all over. The Iara, laughing hard, lay back and stretched out in her perverse giggling, and went on stretching out and out, dissolving, dissolving, and turned into a tongue of white sand. And soon a beautiful palm tree grew into the sky, with two potato-shaped feet at its base. And when the Father of all Cearenses took a look, he'd been cut in half, left with just two little potatoes. The others, Iara planted.

The Cearenses were always much more heroic than their southern brethren, the Gaúchos. But all on account of Iara's wicked trick, they were made exactly like all the other men in this world. That is to say, just a little smaller.

Notes

1. Manuel Bandeira (1886–1968) was, among other things, a modernist poet of the same generation as Mário de Andrade; the two had a long-standing friendship that produced a wrist-straining compendium of lively, impassioned letters.

2. Jean-Baptiste Debret (1768–1848) was among the members of the so-called French Artistic Mission, a group of artists who traveled to Brazil in 1816 at the invitation of the recently transplanted Portuguese court. He remained there for the next fifteen years and produced a slew of depictions of everyday life in Brazil.

3. Luciano Gallet (1893–1931) was a composer and pianist who shared Andrade's enthusiasm for Brazilian folklore.

4. Paulo Prado (1869–1943) was a pioneering participant and patron of the modernist movement in São Paulo and the author of the landmark essay *Portrait of Brazil: An Essay on Brazilian Sadness*, which would be published the year after this trip.

5. José Pereira da Graça Aranha (1868–1931) was an elder statesman of letters, early enthusiast, and would-be head of the burgeoning Brazilian modernist movement, having taken a prominent part in the pioneering Modern Art Week of 1922. Mário de Andrade initially defended him, but in 1926 wrote an open letter calling him a poor, "irritatingly dogmatic" mentor who had joined the modernists "purely out of a desire to lead something." This was their first encounter after the letter.

6. Rodrigo Melo Franco de Andrade (1898–1969) was an art critic and the first director of SPHAN (now IPHAN), the national heritage preservation foundation, which Mário de Andrade would help design in 1936.

7. Ismael Nery (1900–1934) was a proto-surrealist painter. In an essay around this time, Andrade would praise Nery's art but criticize what he saw as a tendency to prioritize symbolic

meaning over technical refinement, leading to somewhat slap-dash work.

8. Joaquim Maria Machado de Assis (1839–1908) was one of Brazil's greatest writers, the author of classics including *The Posthumous Memoirs of Brás Cubas*. Andrade admittedly had an ambiguous relationship with Machado de Assis, admiring his oeuvre while professing dislike for the man himself.

9. Olívia Guedes Penteado (1872–1934) was the heir to a São Paulo coffee-plantation fortune, which she turned toward supporting the arts, modernists in particular. Mário was likely hoping for a repeat of the raucous 1924 trip in which he, fellow modernist Oswald de Andrade, the patron and historian Paulo Prado, the painter Tarsila do Amaral, and the Swiss poet Blaise Cendrars, besides Dona Olívia, traveled to colonial towns in Minas Gerais and were dazzled at their "discovery" of long-neglected Brazilian baroque art. This time around, the intellectuals and artists were replaced by two young women: Olívia's niece, Margarida "Mag" Guedes Nogueira (1908–2011), and Tarsila's daughter, Dulce "Dolur" do Amaral Pinto (1906–1966).

10. Washington Luís Pereira de Sousa (1869–1957) was president of Brazil from 1926 to 1930, the last years of the "First Republic," which was brought to an end by Getúlio Vargas's 1930 coup.

11. The Ilha Fiscal, a palatial customs house perched just offshore in Guanabara Bay, was the site of the last lavish ball before Brazil's imperial monarchy was toppled in 1889 and has thus become an improbable shorthand for opulent celebration on the verge of a fall.

12. Paolo and Francesca are doomed lovers depicted in Dante's *Inferno*, which reminds Andrade of the historian Paulo Prado; Tristão de Ataíde was the pen name used by the writer and critic Alceu Amoroso Lima (1893–1983), which echoes Tristan and Isolde, which leads to the opera of the same name by Richard Wagner (1813–1883); finally, Andrade name-checks the French scholar Gaston Paris (1839–1903) before closing out the list of partygoers with the most famous star-crossed lovers of all time.

13. The author plays around with pseudonyms for the two girls on the trip; an initial version renamed them Eulália and Magnólia.

14. John Graz (1891–1980) was a Swiss artist who settled in São Paulo and participated in the modernist movement there.

15. In the original manuscript, the name Mag is crossed out. Andrade was inspired to rebaptize the two young women after a passenger by the name of Josafá came on board, reminding him

of the Valley of Josaphat, the site of the Last Judgment, the horn blown by the archangel Gabriel, and the scales used by the archangel Michael to weigh the souls of humanity. Nicknames were born: Margarida became Balança, or Scales, Dulce became Trombeta, or Trumpet, and Dona Olívia was secretly dubbed Last Judgment. Andrade censored the last nickname, however, preferring to refer to the coffee-bean heiress throughout the trip as the "Coffee Queen."

16. *Oca* means house or home in Tupi, while *dondoca*—a slang term of uncertain etymology—refers to a lady who lunches.

17. *Coco*, meaning coconut, here designates an Afro-Brazilian musical style typical of the Northeast; an alternative etymology plays off the fact that *coco* can also mean noggin, and coco singers traditionally improvise simple lyrics to go along with the rhythm.

18. Ascenso Ferreira (1895–1965) and Joaquim Inojosa (1901–1987), two members of the Pernambuco circle of modernists.

19. Restaurante Leite, founded in 1882 and the oldest restaurant in Brazil to continually operate from the same address, is still an "inevitability" for tourists wanting a taste of old Recife. The Butantan Institute, a research institution and park in São Paulo, likewise remains a hot ticket for visitors to São Paulo keen on herpetology.

20. The Padaria Espiritual, or Spiritual Bakery, was a literary group in Belle Époque Ceará that published its work in a newspaper fittingly titled *Pão*—"Bread."

21. Tio Pio was Pio Lourenço Corrêa (1875–1957), an older cousin whom Andrade became close to. His farm in Araraquara, São Paulo, would be a refuge for Andrade throughout his life, and was where Andrade wrote the first draft of *Macunaíma*.

22. "Wild green seas of my Native Land . . ." are the opening words of José de Alencar's *Iracema* (1865), translated by Richard and Isabel Burton as *Iracema, the Honey-Lips: A Legend of Brazil*.

23. Francisco Gomes da Silva (1791–1852), known to intimates and history as Chalaça, was a notorious confidant of the young emperor Pedro I of Brazil (1798–1834), serving the monarch as a jack-of-all-trades.

24. Amazonia was gripped by a rubber boom in the late nineteenth century, as the commercial potential of latex became apparent. The age of rubber, and the tremendous prosperity it brought a few in the region, came crashing down in 1912, after rubber-tree seeds smuggled out of the country by the Englishman

Henry Wickham decades earlier and planted in tropical British colonies finally matured, breaking the Amazon's near monopoly on the commodity.

25. A loan word from Guarani meaning large or great.

26. Antônio Frederico de Castro Alves (1847–1871), the Romantic poet known for his volcanically emotive verses.

27. "I-Juca Pirama," in old Tupi, means "he who must be killed." The phrase is the title of a poem by the Romantic poet Gonçalves Dias (1823–1864) that tells the story of a warrior who shames his tribe by begging for mercy in the face of ritual sacrifice and must recover his honor.

28. The battle of the flowers was a Carnival tradition born in Nice of a competition between flower-bedecked carriages; it was transplanted to Brazil in the late nineteenth century as a more sedate and dignified alternative to the popular no-holds-barred *entrudo*.

29. In this little-heralded 1924 Western, synopses inform, the hero journeys west to settle a dispute over oil lands, faces down a crooked foreman, and defends a young lady's honor in the process.

30. Schedules in Belém traditionally revolve around before and after the near-inevitable afternoon cloudburst.

31. Lloyd Brasileiro was a state-owned carrier that ran from 1894 to 1997, when it was dismantled by the government.

32. As far as this translator's taste buds can recall, this description is spot-on.

33. An ironic quotation of the motto of the city of São Paulo, which means "I am not led, I lead."

34. *Mungunzá* or *canjica* is a sweet hominy porridge.

35. *Angélica* is the common name of a few plants in Brazil, among them *Gomphrena globosa*, *Angelica archangelica*, and *Polianthes tuberosa*. In the impossibility of knowing which might have adorned the woman's turban, I imagined the white flowers of the tuberose.

36. Andrade would later lambaste himself for this instinctive comparison between the colors of the hammock in Belém and the palette of the father of Cubism, in a draft of a preface to the diary: *What made me settle on buying that hammock, what made me like it more than any other, wasn't any particular local craft or reasons of greater utility, but the fact that its combination of colors, deep blues and earth tones, was very much like certain intelligent, discreet color combinations used in*

Cubist painting. "A Braque!" I exclaimed, and I bought the hammock. In fact, I've been traveling mainly around myself, selfishly applying my experiences instead of enriching myself with new ones.

37. *Aboio* is the term for the plaintive, often wordless songs sung while herding cattle. In *As melodias do boi*, Andrade observes that this particular song was sung back to him by the poet Jayme Griz. It may be worth recalling that in a hemispheric inversion, the Brazilian South is cooler than the North.

38. Boi bumbá, or bumba meu boi, is a folktale told through song and dance that narrates the death and resurrection of an ox (see note 84).

39. *Caboclo* originated as a term designating Indigenous peoples in Brazil who maintained contact with colonizers and is now used to refer variously to people of Indigenous descent, mixed Indigenous and white descent, and country folk in general.

40. The Paraguayan War, or the War of the Triple Alliance, pitted Brazil, Argentina, and Uruguay against Paraguay in what is still the bloodiest conflict in the region. Between 1864 and 1870, the Alliance wreaked terrible damage on Paraguay, wiping out as much as two-thirds of the population and eventually annexing major swaths of territory. Brazilian losses were vastly smaller but still significant: some fifty thousand men.

41. Virgulino Ferreira da Silva (1897–1938), better known to his contemporaries and history as Lampião (Lantern or Lamp), was the most notorious outlaw in the backlands of Brazil's Northeast, having taken up arms after his father was killed by the police.

42. The contemporary Brazilian phrase for breakfast is *café da manhã* (morning coffee), while the older usage of Portuguese origin is *pequeno almoço* (small lunch). While it is more common in English for adjectives to be placed before nouns, adjectives in Brazilian Portuguese normally follow the noun, but may be inverted for a poetic, somewhat highfalutin effect.

43. In the last chapter of Andrade's epic "rhapsody" *Macunaíma*, published the year after his Amazonian voyage, the (anti)hero goes up into the sky to become part of the *brilho inútil das estrelas*—the useless twinkling of the stars—and is transformed into a constellation.

44. The trip would take Andrade and his companions on board a number of different vessels. *Vaticanos* were the largest and most luxurious steamers; *gaiolas* offered more cramped quarters, which justified locals referring to them as "birdcages." Here,

with the exception of the odd Vatican-related pun, I have glossed them as steamers, for simplicity's sake.

45. The verb *donoliviar* almost certainly appears nowhere else in recorded Portuguese, and with good reason: it's a fanciful adaptation of Dona Olívia's name. Having become familiar with her over the past few pages, readers may imagine for themselves what it would mean to "donoliviate" around.

46. Here, Andrade begins to play off a foundational document in Brazilian history and literature, the letter written by Pêro Vaz de Caminha to the Portuguese king Dom Manuel I, which describes the first encounter between the members of Pedro Álvares Cabral's expedition and Indigenous peoples in 1500. In one interaction, the crew showed the natives "a chicken; they were almost afraid of it and refused to lay hands on it; they then took it as if startled."

47. Now also referred to as "old Tupi," *Abanheenga* was the Tupi-Guarani word for their language at the time of colonization.

48. Andrade is a common surname in Brazil, and Senator Andrade (1862–1953), who came to own around three million hectares of land in the region, was no relation to the author.

49. The modernist painter Tarsila do Amaral and the author Oswald de Andrade, also no relation, whom Mário would dearly have liked to have had along on his Amazonian journey. Later, after a series of homophobic insults from Oswald, Mário would strike references to his onetime friend from the manuscript.

50. Tapuio is a term derived from Tupi and used by the Portuguese to refer to any Indigenous groups who did not speak Tupi; it later became a catchall term for detribalized Indigenous peoples, and Andrade uses it generically.

51. Andrade continues to play indirectly off Pêro Vaz de Caminha's pioneering description of Indigenous peoples in Brazil. In one passage, Caminha writes: "Walking among them were three or four young women, quite young and quite gracious, their hair black and long down their backs, and their private parts so prominent and neat and so clean of hairs that, look as we might, they felt no shame."

52. The folktale goes as follows: A tribe was reduced to one brother and one sister, and she began visiting his hammock in the dark of night to make love with him, always disappearing before dawn. The brother eventually decided to streak his mysterious lover with red urucum (annatto) and black genipap dyes so he would know her by daylight. Once found out, the sister planted

a seed and grew a staggeringly tall liana that led her up to the firmament, where she became the moon—her face still streaked with the marks of her transgression. Macunaíma uses the same sort of liana to clamber up to the heavens at the end of his own saga.

53. *Parintintin* is actually the Munduruku word for enemy, but was used for decades to designate the Kawahib people.

54. *Paroara* is a slang term from the period, derived from the popular name for birds that abandoned drought-stricken lands and used to refer to those who migrated from the Brazilian Northeast, mostly from the state of Ceará, to Amazonia in search of work.

55. For a decade or so after its birth, Brazilian modernism would be persistently confused with futurism and asked to answer for its stances. Andrade vocally distanced himself from the latter, which spared him being present at a recital by Filippo Tommaso Marinetti in São Paulo, where the founder of the futurist movement was booed and pelted with all manner of produce, but did not spare him ribbing by this group of intellectuals in Manaus.

56. According to perhaps more reliable sources, the girls have the hair removed only from their scalps.

57. *Uapé* is the Tupi word for a water lily—it's unclear what bird Andrade was referring to here.

58. *Cabroeira*, derived from *cabra*, goat, means a group of goats, and the scuffling confusion derived thereof. In the Brazilian Northeast, *cabra* is also used in the sense of guy or fellow.

59. This water lily, the largest of its kind, with leaves up to ten feet across, was originally baptized *Victoria regia* in honor of Queen Victoria, and is still referred to in Portuguese as *vitória-régia*, but has since been rebaptized *Victoria amazonica*.

60. Pacaás Novos is the name given today to a river and a mountain range in the state of Rondônia, and has been used to describe an Indigenous group that was spotted on the bank of the river Pakaa Nova in the late eighteenth century who call themselves Wari', a word in their language meaning *us* or *we*. As of the 1920s, the Pacaás Novos had been largely isolated and Brazilians knew little of them. However, the group described here, as readers will quickly note, is fictitious.

61. *Bacororô* is the term used for a traditional dance of the Bororo people.

62. *Marubixaba* or *morubixaba* are among terms used in the Amazonian region to designate a chief.

63. *Pajé* is a term used to designate a member of the tribe who performs healing or shamanic functions.

64. The exchange of flowers as a means to communicate sentiments is not an exact science. One contemporary dictionary of the language of flowers indicates that French lavender, as a response to a scarlet carnation, would mean "I feel very much the same"; another codes scarlet carnation as "vivid, pure passion" and French lavender as religious devotion; and yet another lists a deep red carnation as "Alas, my poor heart!" and lavender as "Distrust."

65. Ursa Major is visible only in the northern reaches of Brazil, closer to the equator. In Brazilian folklore, the Saci is a one-legged trickster, a Black boy in a red hat; tipping your head, you'll find it easy to imagine the tail of the Big Dipper as the Saci's lone leg.

66. The ciranda, its name derived from a Portuguese round dance, took an unusual turn in the region around Tefé (Amazonas) and morphed into a dramatic rendition of a story in which a hunter kills a bird (a carão, or limpkin) and is called to task by the community, is brought in to confess, and sees the priest resurrect the wounded bird.

67. Andrade was intrigued by the name of the town, which literally means "The End of Evils," and made a point of visiting it. The community, now known as Atalaia do Norte, reportedly got its original name when a long-suffering migrant settled on the riverbank and, feeling that he had put a dark spell behind him, nailed up a sign deeming his new home "the end" of his tribulations.

68. The song Andrade quotes here was originally "Sweet Little Caraboo," a 1904 pastiche of a Native American legend that began as a Broadway song and was adapted into Portuguese as "Ó minha caraboo" in 1913, becoming an earworm at that year's carnival.

69. The Baedeker Guides were invaluable companions for tourists for the better part of a century, becoming synonymous with travel guides in general.

70. "Parrot's beak" seems to have occurred to many peoples at many times as an apt descriptor for a whole range of colorful plants, from poinsettias to trees to blooms in the Canary Islands and shrubs in the Philippines. Since Andrade's specimen has been lost to time, the reader is invited to imagine her own parrot's-beak bloom.

71. Manuel Maria Barbosa du Bocage (1765–1805) was a Portuguese writer known for his cutting, subversive poetry; Andrade plays off the poet's surname here and in other works with the word *bocagem*, derived from *boca* (mouth) and meaning a swear word.

72. Leticia was ceded by the Peruvian government to Colombia in a treaty ratified in 1928, although it was briefly recaptured by patriotic-minded Peruvians in a short-lived war in 1932; it has been a part of Colombia ever since.

73. The leper colony at San Pablo de Loreto had been established just a few years earlier, in 1925, and would accept patients through the late 1960s—during which time a young Che Guevara spent a spell as a volunteer.

74. In the late nineteenth century, the discovery that deposits of guano and nitrates in the Atacama Desert could be a rich source of fertilizer provoked something like a gold rush. Chile took up arms against Bolivia and Peru from 1879 to 1884, in what is known variously as the War of the Pacific, the Saltpeter War, or the Ten Cents War. A victorious Chile occupied Lima for several years, ultimately took one Peruvian province, Tarapacá, and held the rest of the Atacama, cutting Bolivia off from the sea.

75. "Plant cotton and coffee; work the rubber"—presumably an official encouragement to the workers of Iquitos.

76. Mosquitoes, for all their ubiquity and their varieties, go by many names in Portuguese: besides *mosquito*, there's *pernilongo* or *pernalonga* (literally, "long legs"), *carapanã*, and *muriçoca*, to name a few. In Iquitos, Andrade was able to add the Spanish *zancudo* to his vocabulary.

77. "Cold chicha, one real." Chicha is a drink of Indigenous origin present across much of Latin America, and hence with any number of base ingredients and variations, both alcoholic and nonalcoholic. Andrade compares it unfavorably to aluá, which is a fermented beverage, something of a Brazilian cousin to chicha: it is commonly made from either corn or pineapple.

78. Andrade transcribes a few store signs: António Bardales's carpentry shop goes by the Latin moniker Modus Vivendi, while Juan Chiong, presumably of Chinese origin, has used the Spanish Zapatería to designate his shoe store.

79. *Tuxaua* and *morubixaba*, among other variations, are terms derived from Tupi that designate a chief or community leader.

80. "If you want [a picture], you have to pay!"

81. Marajoara is the name attributed to a pre-Columbian civilization that thrived for centuries on Marajó Island, best known for their colorful patterned ceramic arts.

82. Guiomar Novaes (1894–1979) was a renowned Brazilian pianist.

83. Vanadiol was the name of a blood tonic sold at the time that promised to cure everything from tuberculosis to indigestion.

84. The story told in the bumba meu boi or boi bumbá is essentially as follows: Francisco and Catirina (or Catarina) are an enslaved couple living on a Portuguese man's plantation. Catirina becomes pregnant—hence the name "Mãe Catirina" (Mother Catirina)—and gets a craving for an ox tongue. As is often the case in such tales, the craving is both specific and inconvenient: she needs to eat the tongue of the master's favorite ox. Francisco obliges, secretly killing the ox. Cazumbá, traditionally one of the most elaborate costumes in the pageant, is a playful, often grotesque-looking spirit that swoops down to scare Francisco as he is committing the act. Once the crime is found out, the master demands that Francisco resurrect the animal or die himself, and the ox is eventually brought back to life by the pajé, a shaman.

85. "Give me your hand so you don't fall." "Of course." "Help yourself."

86. In Brazilian folklore, Iara is the name of a siren who lures men to their deaths.

87. Herbert de Azevedo, the mayor of Coari, was felled in a shootout in late June 1927. The discontented locals, however, were quick to clarify that they hadn't meant to kill the poor mayor and had attacked City Hall only in hopes of killing the prosecutor and the police chief (both of whom escaped).

88. An excerpt from the cordel poem "O povo na cruz" (The Common Man Crucified), a lament of poverty and inequality that was among the folk poetry in Andrade's collection.

89. A few years later, Lindoso would be brutally murdered by local residents—after, the story goes, he took their papers under false pretenses and laid claim to their lands.

90. Lo Schiavo (The Slave) is an opera by the Brazilian composer Antônio Carlos Gomes (1836–1896), first performed in 1889, most famous for its orchestral depiction of a dawn.

91. These are folk rhymes of Portuguese origin; while English doesn't employ rhymes for calling backgammon rolls, bingo makes up for it—sixes may be "Tom Mix" or "chopping sticks,"

ten may be "cock and hen" or "Uncle Ben," and so on—and I have borrowed a few such rhymes here.

92. The Portuguese measure of depth used here is *braça*; there is a whole corresponding vocabulary in American English derived from sounding calls on the Mississippi River, from which the writer Mark Twain derived his pen name—"mark twain" being the call for two fathoms, or twelve feet. Since the Portuguese sounding calls are more immediately intelligible to the layman, I have adapted them here rather than use their Mississippi equivalents.

93. In the original, the first mate says the ship is *safo* (has made it), mirroring the Portuguese spelling of Sappho.

94. The Madeira-Mamoré railway line saw so many workers die during multiple attempts at construction that it became known as the "Devil's Railroad." It was built to ease rubber exports from western Brazil and Bolivia; tragically, it was finished just as the Amazonian rubber monopoly was broken and has long since been deactivated.

95. Here, Andrade reels off a cast of notable immigrants to Brazil: Líbero Badaró (an Italian-born Brazilian liberal politician, assassinated in 1830), Nicolas-Antoine Taunay (a French painter who founded Rio's Academia de Belas Artes), Dom João VI (the Portuguese king who fled Napoleon and moved his court to Rio), and Francesco Matarazzo (an Italian immigrant who built a small industrial empire in São Paulo).

96. A reference to *The Naturalist on the River Amazons*, by Henry Walter Bates (1825–1892).

97. The "clock" train, or *trem "horário,"* was the train that arrived and departed "by the clock"—at predetermined times.

98. Carlos de Morais Andrade (1889–1968), Mário's older brother.

99. To mean something easily dispatched, as in the English "pie" or "cake," or "small potatoes" or "small beer." Andrade notes later, parenthetically: "Back then, the expression *café-pequeno* hadn't become common down South. Or at least I hadn't heard it."

100. The striped cuckoo has dozens of folk names in Portuguese, but the one Andrade uses here is *sem-fim*—"no end."

101. S-120 was a type of imported linen, the epitome of tropical elegance at the time. In Jorge Amado's 1930 novel *Dona Flor and Her Two Husbands*, a character asks for eggshell white S-120 linen for a suit, describing it as "the best on the market." Andrade himself had the clothes he ordered in Belém made from S-120.

102. Amazonas, a state drenched with rain and crisscrossed with rivers, is not known for its overland transportation. The highway Andrade refers to, which would be built only under the dictatorship in the 1960s and '70s, has since fallen into muddy decay. Its maintenance is stunningly challenging and continues to affect the environment and Indigenous peoples in the surrounding areas. No word on what remains of the Olívia Penteado Station, inaugurated half a century before the highway itself.

103. The Amazon knife or Mesquita knife was developed by the Portuguese immigrant José Cláudio de Mesquita, the idea being to use a sort of blade that would damage the rubber trees less than the traditional hand axes used to harvest latex.

104. The Baré people, who live along the upper Negro River and the Xié River, have had their name become synonymous with the people of the state of Amazonas in general.

105. "They don't need any more music, monsieur! They've gone to bed!"

106. This entry was written post-1940 and marked for insertion at this point in the manuscript. There follows a draft of a letter, half in Portuguese and half in French, addressed to the "communist Jewish friend," Dina Lévi-Strauss, who came to Brazil with her husband, Claude, and worked alongside him at the University of São Paulo.

107. By "hybridism," Andrade means the name of the lake—José Açu—a Portuguese name and a Tupi adjective meaning large.

108. The speaker "Frenchifies" the Portuguese words *jararaca* (a kind of viper), *então* (then), and *canivete* (jackknife), among a few others.

109. Andrade strings together a motley list of rhyming plants and animals: *pirarucu* (a fabulously large river fish), *jacaré* (caiman), *jacamim* (trumpeter bird), *jacu* (guan bird), *cajá* (hog plum), *maracajá* (margay or tree ocelot), and *tracajá* (a kind of river turtle).

110. Andrade's traveling companion is, for chronologically obvious reasons, not the Romantic writer Alfred de Musset (1810–1857).

111. The buffaloes that have become a part of the scenery on Marajó Island and elsewhere in Pará are actually Asian water buffaloes.

112. Herons, yes; jacanas, no.

113. Tragically, this seems to have happened on multiple occasions at the dawn of São Paulo's football leagues: São Paulo Athletic beat Paulistano in the finals 4–0 in 1902, 2–1 in 1903, and 1–0 in 1904. Happily for fans of Paulistano (now São Paulo FC), São Paulo Athletic's football team no longer exists.

114. Graça Aranha is the writer with whom Andrade had an uncomfortable run-in at the start of his journey (see note 5). Andrade is getting in a little dig at Graça Aranha's notion, put forth in the 1921 book *A estética da vida*, that the individual must become one with the "Universal Whole." In a letter to Manuel Bandeira, Andrade described the book as "a ragbag of Oriental philosophies."

115. The capital of the state of Paraíba, which then went by the same name, was changed to João Pessoa in 1930 in honor of an assassinated governor and vice-presidential candidate.

116. The phrase means "for the use of the Dauphin" and refers to editions bowdlerized for the benefit of younger audiences—or second-rate editions in general.

117. Andrade, who had systematically replaced the girls' nicknames (Mag and Dolur) with Scales and Trumpet, slips here at the end, perhaps restoring Dolur's name once she's reunited with her mother, Tarsila, and off the ship.

118. Sebastiana Campos, or Bastiana, was the cook at Mário de Andrade's home.

119. Andrade's notes include an excerpt from Richard Burton's book *The Highlands of the Brazil*, describing a cave in Paulo Afonso, Bahia, known as the "Vampire's Grot. Its appearance is singular. The entrance, instead of being low, after the fashion of caverns, is a tall parallelogrammic portal leaning a little to the south. Hence it has its Saintess (uma Santa) who shows herself at times, and the people have heard martial music, and singing which did not, they judged, proceed from mortal wind-pipe."

120. The "Juazeiro" allusion is probably a reference to the series of events begun in 1889 when Padre Cícero, a priest worshipped as a folk saint, gave communion to a young woman named Maria de Araújo and the wafer reportedly turned to blood in her mouth. The alleged miracle sparked a flood of pilgrimages and gave Cícero a reputation as a miracle worker.

121. José Albano (1882–1923) was indeed a poet from Ceará, known for his European sojourns and a self-aggrandizing streak, although perhaps not to the extent described here.

122. Cearenses—the demonym for those from the then province, now state of Ceará—were chief among the Paroaras, migrants from the Brazilian Northeast who flocked to Amazonia during a punishing series of droughts, many recruited into debt slavery. In common and often pejorative parlance, *Cearense* was used indiscriminately for all such migrants.

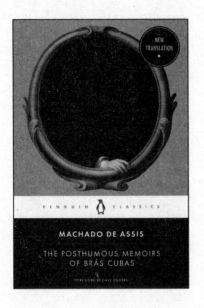

The Violent Land

The siren song of the lush, cocoa-rich forests of Bahia lures them all—the adventurers, the gamblers, the brave and beautiful women. It is not a gentle song, but a song of greed, madness, and blood most cannot resist until it is too late—not Margot, the prostitute who comes for love; not Cabral, the unscrupulous lawyer; and not Juca, whose quest to reap the jungle's harvest plants the seeds of his own ruin.

PENGUIN CLASSICS

Ready to find your next great classic? Let us help. Visit prh.com/penguinclassics

Backlands

The Canudos Campaign

Written by a former army lieutenant, civil engineer, and journalist, *Backlands* is Euclides da Cunha's portrayal of Brazil's infamous War of Canudos during the 1890s. The conflict was between the government and the village of Canudos in the northeastern state of Bahia. Far from just an objective retelling, da Cunha's story shows both the significance of this event and the complexities of Brazilian society.